HTML5

Made Easy

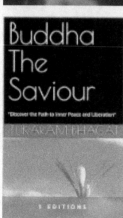

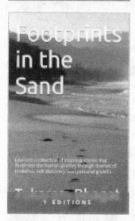

Copyright Statement

Tukaram Bhagat

Author | Trainer | Coach | Mentor

Mumbai, Maharashtra, India
Mobile & WhatsApp No: +91 7045364977
Email: tcbhagat@rediffmail.com

Published in 2024 by Bhagat Publishing, Amazon Kindle @ USA

Imprint: Independently published

First Edition

About the Author

Tukaram Bhagat is a seasoned professional with over 21 years of extensive experience in the fields of Information Technology, Machine Learning, Programming, and Artificial Intelligence. With a diverse skill set encompassing Programming, Web Development, Mobile Apps Development, and Teaching, Mentoring, Coaching, and Guiding, he has established himself as a versatile expert in the tech industry.

Having earned an MBA in Information Technology and a bachelor's degree in Computer Applications, Tukaram further honed his expertise with an Honours Diploma in Systems Management from NIIT, MS-CIT from MKCL, and certifications in ITIL, MCP, MCTS, Business Success Coaching, and Diploma in Cyber Laws. His academic background is complemented by hands-on experience gained from working in various capacities, including IT Trainer, Centre Manager, and Manager for Training Delivery.

Tukaram's professional journey has taken him across borders, as he has worked in India, Dominica, and Costa Rica, gaining valuable insights and exposure to diverse cultures and work environments. Throughout his career, he has impacted the lives of thousands of students through his teaching and mentoring endeavours, both in India and abroad. His pedagogical prowess extends across various domains, including Java, .NET, and open-source technologies. His adeptness in training methodologies, coupled with his innate ability to mentor and coach, has earned him admiration and respect within the IT fraternity.

Renowned for his ability to simplify complex subjects and present them in a clear, easy-to-understand manner, Tukaram is committed to demystifying technology and making it accessible to people worldwide. His dedication to this cause is reflected in his tenure with esteemed organizations such as Megahertz Business Systems, LCC Infotech Limited, S3 Computer Education, kaRROX Technologies, TalentEdge, and Aptech Limited.

With a passion for empowering individuals with technological knowledge and skills, Tukaram continues to be a guiding force in the ever-evolving landscape of Information

Technology. His unwavering commitment to making technology approachable and understandable underscores his role as a leader and influencer in the industry.

In addition to his illustrious career in Information Technology, Tukaram has also made significant contributions as an author, penning several acclaimed books that span diverse topics. His literary works include "Life's Blueprint," a thought-provoking exploration of timeless wisdom for a fulfilling journey; "Mastering NumPy," a comprehensive guide to unlocking the full potential of this powerful Python library; "Buddha The Saviour," an insightful reflection on the life and teachings of the revered spiritual leader; "Rising from the Rubble," a compelling narrative of resilience and hope in the face of adversity; and "Artificially Intelligent World," a visionary exploration of the impact of AI on society and humanity. Through his writing, Tukaram continues to inspire, educate, and enlighten readers around the globe, cementing his legacy as a multifaceted thought leader and visionary author.

Beyond his professional endeavours, Tukaram remains committed to sharing his knowledge and expertise through his role as an author. His insightful publications serve as guiding beacons for IT enthusiasts, providing invaluable insights into the ever-evolving landscape of Information Technology.

As Tukaram Bhagat continues to push the boundaries of innovation and excellence in IT, his journey serves as an inspiration to aspiring technologists worldwide. With his unwavering dedication, unparalleled expertise, and visionary leadership, Tukaram remains at the forefront of shaping the future of Information Technology.

Thank you.

Books by Author

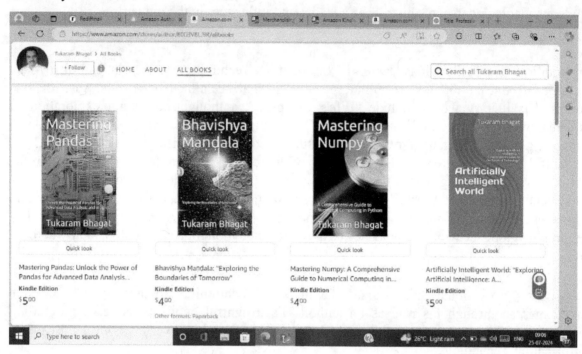

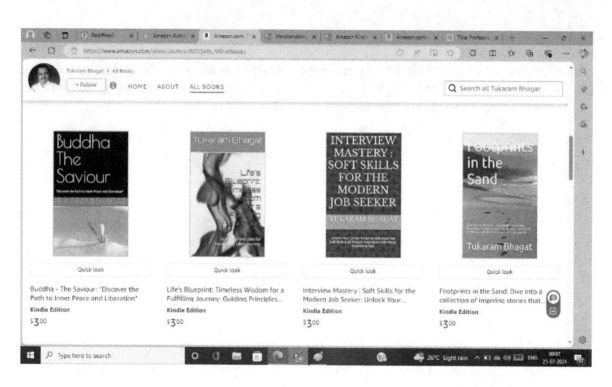

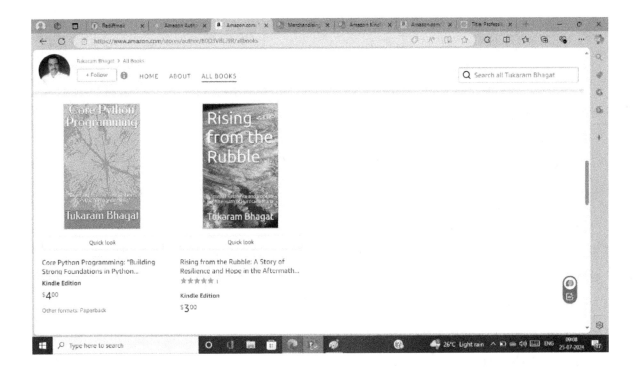

Quick look   Quick look

Core Python Programming: "Building   Rising from the Rubble: A Story of
Strong Foundations in Python...   Resilience and Hope in the Aftermath...
                                            ★★★★★ 1
Kindle Edition
$4.00   **Kindle Edition**
                                            $3.00
Other formats: Paperback

Table of Contents

Preface

Welcome to "HTML5 Made Easy," a comprehensive guide designed to introduce you to the world of HTML5, the cornerstone of modern web development. Whether you are a beginner just starting your journey in web development or an experienced developer looking to update your knowledge, this book is structured to provide you with a thorough understanding of HTML5 and its powerful features.

Table of Contents

Equip yourself with the knowledge to set up a productive development environment, including the installation and use of text editors and local servers.

7. Installing and Using Text Editors

Explore various text editors, understand their features, and find the one that best suits your development style.

8. Setting Up a Local Server

Learn how to set up a local server to test your HTML5 projects efficiently.

9. Understanding the Structure of an HTML5 Document

Get acquainted with the basic structure of an HTML5 document and its essential components.

10. HTML5 Document Structure

Deepen your understanding of the elements that constitute an HTML5 document, starting with the Doctype declaration.

11. Doctype Declaration

Understand the importance of the Doctype declaration and how it ensures proper rendering of HTML5 documents.

12. Text Formatting and Semantics

Master the use of headings, paragraphs, and other semantic elements to create well-structured and meaningful web content.

13. Working with Links and Lists

Learn to create effective navigation using links and organize information using lists.

14. Images and Media

Discover the best practices for using images and media in your web pages, including formats and optimization techniques.

15. HTML5 Forms and Input Types

Explore the new and enhanced features of HTML5 forms, including new input types and built-in validation.

16. Canvas and SVG

Unleash your creativity with the Canvas API and Scalable Vector Graphics (SVG) for creating dynamic and interactive graphics.

17. Geolocation API

Implement location-based services in your web pages using the Geolocation API, while considering privacy and security.

18. Web Storage

Understand the different types of web storage and how to use them to enhance user experience and application performance.

19. CSS3 and HTML5

Learn how to style your HTML5 documents using CSS3 for visually appealing and responsive designs.

20. JavaScript and HTML5

Integrate JavaScript with HTML5 to create dynamic and interactive web applications.

21. HTML5 Best Practices and Performance

Adopt best practices for writing clean, maintainable, and performant HTML5 code.

22. SEO and HTML5

Optimize your HTML5 web pages for search engines to improve visibility and ranking.

23. Performance Optimization

Learn techniques to optimize the performance of your HTML5 web applications.

24. Projects and Case Studies

Apply your knowledge through practical projects and case studies, including building a responsive website.

25. HTML5 Game Development

Explore the exciting world of HTML5 game development with practical examples.

26. Real-World Case Studies

Gain insights from real-world applications of HTML5 across different industries.

27. Future of HTML5

Look ahead to the future developments and trends in HTML5 technology.

28. Resources and Further Learning

Access additional resources and suggestions for further learning to continue your journey in web development.

This book is more than just a tutorial; it is a comprehensive guide that will equip you with the knowledge and skills to create modern, responsive, and dynamic web applications using HTML5. I hope you find this book both informative and inspiring, and that it serves as a valuable resource in your web development endeavors.

Happy coding!

Sincerely,

Tukaram Bhagat

Author | Coach | Mentor | Trainer

Introduction to HTML5

- ✓ **Overview of HTML5**
- ✓ **Evolution of HTML**
- ✓ **HTML5 Specifications and Features**
- ✓ **Importance and Benefits of HTML5**

Overview of HTML5

HTML5 is the fifth and current major version of the Hypertext Markup Language (HTML), the standard language used for structuring and presenting content on the web. It was designed to improve the language with support for the latest multimedia while keeping it easily readable by humans and consistently understood by computers and devices, such as web browsers.

Key Features of HTML5:

1. New Elements and Attributes:

Semantic Elements: `<header>`, `<footer>`, `<article>`, `<section>`, and `<nav>` help structure the content of web pages in a more meaningful way.

Form Elements: New input types like `<input type="email">`, `<input type="date">`, `<input type="range">`, and attributes like `placeholder`, `required`, and `pattern` improve form usability and validation.

2. Multimedia Support:

Audio and Video: `<audio>` and `<video>` tags allow embedding of multimedia content without needing third-party plugins like Flash.

Canvas Element: `<canvas>` enables drawing graphics on the fly using JavaScript.

3. APIs and DOM Interfaces:

Geolocation API: Allows web applications to access the user's geographical location.

Web Storage API: Provides a way to store data locally within the user's browser (localStorage and sessionStorage).

Web Workers: Allows background scripts to run without blocking the user interface.

Web Sockets: Provides full-duplex communication channels over a single TCP connection.

4. Improved Parsing Rules:

Error Handling: Enhanced parsing algorithms make it easier for browsers to interpret and render HTML content, even if it's poorly written.

5. Deprecated Elements and Attributes:

Elements like `<font>`, `<center>`, and attributes like `align`, `bgcolor`, are either deprecated or removed in favor of CSS.

6.Accessibility:

Improved support for assistive technologies, making web content more accessible to people with disabilities.

HTML5 aims to enhance user experience by providing richer and more interactive content, improving compatibility across different browsers and devices, and simplifying the development process for web developers.

Evolution of HTML

HTML, or HyperText Markup Language, has been the backbone of web development since its inception. Its evolution reflects the ever-changing demands of web development and user experience. The evolution can be categorized into several phases:

HTML 1.0 (1991): The original HTML specification by Tim Berners-Lee introduced the fundamental elements for creating web pages, such as headings, paragraphs, links, and images. It laid the groundwork for the web as we know it.

HTML 2.0 (1995): This version formalized the elements and attributes introduced in HTML 1.0 and added new features, including forms for user input and tables for data presentation. It was the first widely adopted standard for web development.

HTML 3.2 (1997): HTML 3.2 added support for style sheets, scripting languages (like JavaScript), and improved table handling. It aimed to make web pages more dynamic and visually appealing.

HTML 4.0 (1999): HTML 4.0 introduced a more structured approach to web design, with the inclusion of new elements for improved separation of content and presentation. It also emphasized the importance of web accessibility and internationalization.

HTML 4.01 (2000): This was a minor update to HTML 4.0, providing fixes and improvements while maintaining the core structure.

HTML5 (2014): HTML5 represents a significant leap forward, introducing a wide array of new features and elements designed to enhance web functionality, accessibility, and multimedia integration.

HTML5 Specifications and Features

HTML5 is a comprehensive revision of the HTML standard, designed to address the needs of modern web applications and to simplify the development process. Key specifications and features include:

Semantic Elements: HTML5 introduces new semantic elements that provide meaning to the structure of a web page. Examples include `<header>`, `<footer>`, `<article>`, and `<section>`. These elements help organize content logically and improve accessibility.

```html
<header>
  <h1>Welcome to My Website</h1>
</header>
<section>
  <h2>About Us</h2>
  <p>We are a team of dedicated professionals...</p>
</section>
<footer>
  <p>&copy; 2024 My Website</p>
</footer>
```

Multimedia Support: HTML5 provides native support for audio and video elements through the `<audio>` and `<video>` tags, eliminating the need for third-party plugins like Flash.

```html
<video controls>
  <source src="movie.mp4" type="video/mp4">
  Your browser does not support the video tag.
</video>
```

Form Enhancements: HTML5 enhances form handling with new input types, such as `email`, `date`, and `range`, which provide built-in validation and improve user experience.

```html
<input type="email" name="user_email" placeholder="Enter your email">
<input type="date" name="birthdate">
<input type="range" name="volume" min="0" max="100">
```

Local Storage: HTML5 introduces `localStorage` and `sessionStorage`, which allow web applications to store data on the client side, enhancing performance and enabling offline functionality.

```javascript
// Storing data
localStorage.setItem('username', 'JohnDoe');


// Retrieving data
var username = localStorage.getItem('username');
```

Canvas and SVG: HTML5 includes the `<canvas>` element for drawing graphics on the fly via JavaScript, and it supports Scalable Vector Graphics (SVG) for high-quality, resolution-independent images.

```html
<canvas id="myCanvas" width="200" height="100"></canvas>
<script>
 var canvas = document.getElementById('myCanvas');
 var ctx = canvas.getContext('2d');
 ctx.fillStyle = 'red';
 ctx.fillRect(10, 10, 150, 75);
```

Importance and Benefits of HTML5

HTML5 is crucial for modern web development due to its wide array of benefits:

Improved User Experience: HTML5's new elements and multimedia features enhance the user experience by providing richer content and smoother interactions without relying on external plugins.

Better Performance: Native support for multimedia and local storage reduces the need for external resources, leading to faster load times and improved performance.

Enhanced Accessibility: Semantic elements and improved form handling contribute to better accessibility, making web content more usable for people with disabilities.

Cross-Platform Compatibility: HTML5 ensures consistent behavior across different devices and browsers, promoting a more uniform experience for users.

Future-Proofing: HTML5 addresses many of the limitations of previous versions and aligns with modern web standards, making it a future-proof choice for web development.

HTML5 represents a major advancement in web technology, offering new features and improvements that cater to the needs of contemporary web development. Its emphasis on semantic structure, multimedia integration, and client-side storage contributes to a richer, more efficient web experience.

Q. 1: HTML5 is the ___ major version of the Hypertext Markup Language.

   a) Third

   b) Fourth

   c) Fifth

   d) Sixth

Answer: c) Fifth

Q. 2: Which of the following is a new semantic element introduced in HTML5?

   a) <div>

   b) <span>

   c) <article>

   d) <table>

Answer: c) <article>

Q. 3: Which HTML5 tag is used to embed video content?

   a) <embed>

   b) <object>

   c) <video>

   d) <media>

Answer: c) <video>

Q. 4: Which new input type in HTML5 is used to enter an email address?

   a) <input type="text">

   b) <input type="email">

   c) <input type="url">

   d) <input type="search">

Answer: b) <input type="email">

Q. 5: The Geolocation API in HTML5 is used to:

a) Draw graphics on a webpage

b) Store data locally within the user's browser

c) Access the user's geographical location

d) Provide full-duplex communication channels over a single TCP connection

Answer: c) Access the user's geographical location

Q. 6: Which HTML5 feature provides a way to store data on the client side?

a) Cookies

b) Web Storage API

c) Cache Manifest

d) Web Sockets

Answer: b) Web Storage API

Q. 7: The <canvas> element in HTML5 is used for:

a) Storing data

b) Embedding videos

c) Drawing graphics

d) Styling content

Answer: c) Drawing graphics

Q. 8: Which of the following elements is deprecated in HTML5?

a) <header>

b) <footer>

c) <font>

d) <section>

Answer: c) <font>

Q. 9: HTML5 enhanced parsing algorithms make it easier for browsers to:

a) Block user interfaces

b) Embed multimedia content

c) Interpret and render HTML content

d) Draw graphics

Answer: c) Interpret and render HTML content

Q. 10: HTML5 improves support for assistive technologies to make web content more accessible to:

a) Developers

b) Browsers

c) Search engines

d) People with disabilities

Answer: d) People with disabilities

2. Setting Up the Development Environment

- ✓ **Installing and Using Text Editors**
- ✓ **Setting Up a Local Server**
- ✓ **Understanding the Structure of an HTML5 Document**

Installing and Using Text Editors

A text editor is an essential tool for writing and editing HTML code. Various text editors are available, each with its own features and capabilities. Here are steps to install and use some popular text editors:

Visual Studio Code (VS Code):

1. Download and Install: Visit the **(https://code.visualstudio.com/)** and download the installer for your operating system (Windows, macOS, or Linux). Run the installer and follow the on-screen instructions.

2. Basic Usage: Open VS Code. You can create a new file by clicking on `File > New File` or by using the shortcut `Ctrl + N` (Windows/Linux) or `Cmd + N` (macOS). Save the file with a `.html` extension, e.g., `index.html`. Start writing your HTML code.

```html
<!DOCTYPE html>
<html>
 <head>
  <title>My First HTML Document</title>
 </head>
 <body>
  <h1>Hello, World!</h1>
  <p>Welcome to HTML5 development.</p>
 </body>
</html>
```

3. Extensions: VS Code supports extensions for enhanced functionality. For HTML development, you can install extensions like "HTML Snippets" for code completion or "Live Server" to preview your HTML file in a browser.

Sublime Text:

1. Download and Install: Go to the (https://www.sublimetext.com/) and download the installer. Install the program following the provided instructions.

2. Basic Usage: Open Sublime Text. Create a new file by selecting `File > New File` or using `Ctrl + N` (Windows/Linux) or `Cmd + N` (macOS). Save the file with a `.html` extension.

```html
<!DOCTYPE html>
<html>
 <head>
  <title>My First HTML Document</title>
 </head>
 <body>
  <h1>Hello, World!</h1>
  <p>Welcome to HTML5 development.</p>
 </body>
</html>
```

3. Packages: Sublime Text offers packages for extended functionality. Install packages like "Emmet" for faster HTML and CSS coding or "LiveServer" to view your changes in real-time.

Notepad++:

1. Download and Install: Visit the [Notepad++ website](https://notepad-plus-plus.org/) and download the installer. Follow the installation process.

2. Basic Usage: Open Notepad++. Create a new document with `File > New` or `Ctrl + N`. Save the file with a `.html` extension.

```
<!DOCTYPE html>
<html>
 <head>
  <title>My First HTML Document</title>
 </head>
 <body>
  <h1>Hello, World!</h1>
  <p>Welcome to HTML5 development.</p>
 </body>
</html>
```

3. Plugins: Notepad++ supports plugins for additional features. You can install plugins like "NppFTP" for FTP access or "Emmet" for quicker coding.

Setting Up a Local Server

A local server allows you to test and view your HTML files as if they were hosted on a web server. Here's how to set up a local server using different tools:

Using Live Server Extension in VS Code:

1. Install Live Server Extension: Open VS Code and go to the Extensions view by clicking on the Extensions icon in the sidebar or pressing `Ctrl + Shift + X` (Windows/Linux) or `Cmd + Shift + X` (macOS). Search for "Live Server" and click `Install`.

2. Run Live Server: Open your HTML file in VS Code. Right-click inside the editor and select "Open with Live Server," or click the "Go Live" button in the bottom-right corner of the VS Code window. Your default web browser will open with a live preview of your HTML file.

Using XAMPP:

1. Download and Install: Visit the (https://www.apachefriends.org/index.html) and download the installer for your operating system. Run the installer and follow the instructions to install XAMPP.

2. Start Apache Server: Open the XAMPP Control Panel and click "Start" next to Apache. This starts the local web server.

3. Place Your Files: Copy your HTML files to the `htdocs` directory inside the XAMPP installation folder (e.g., `C:\xampp\htdocs\` on Windows).

4. Access Your Files: Open your web browser and navigate to `http://localhost/filename.html` to view your HTML file.

Using MAMP:

1. Download and Install: Go to the [MAMP website](https://www.mamp.info/en/) and download the installer for your operating system. Install MAMP following the provided instructions.

2. Start Servers: Open MAMP and click "Start Servers." This starts the Apache and MySQL servers.

3. Place Your Files: Copy your HTML files to the `htdocs` directory within the MAMP installation folder (e.g., `/Applications/MAMP/htdocs/` on macOS).

4. Access Your Files: Open your web browser and navigate to `http://localhost/filename.html` to view your HTML file.

Understanding the Structure of an HTML5 Document

An HTML5 document follows a specific structure that defines how web content is organized and displayed. Here's a breakdown of the key components:

Doctype Declaration:

The `<!DOCTYPE html>` declaration defines the document type and version of HTML. It ensures that the browser renders the page in standards mode.

```
<!DOCTYPE html>
```

HTML Element:

The `<html>` element is the root element that wraps all other elements in the document. It includes the `lang` attribute to specify the language of the document.

```
<html lang="en">
```

Head Section:

The `<head>` section contains meta-information about the document, such as the title, character encoding, and links to stylesheets and scripts.

```
<head>
  <meta charset="UTF-8">
```

```
<meta name="viewport" content="width=device-width, initial-scale=1.0">

<title>Document Title</title>

<link rel="stylesheet" href="styles.css">

</head>
```

Body Section:

The `<body>` section contains the visible content of the web page, including headings, paragraphs, images, links, and other elements.

```
<body>

<header>

 <h1>Main Heading</h1>

</header>

<section>

 <h2>Subheading</h2>

 <p>This is a paragraph.</p>

</section>

<footer>

 <p>Footer content goes here.</p>

</footer>

</body>
```

Example HTML5 Document:

```html
<!DOCTYPE html>
<html lang="en">
 <head>
  <meta charset="UTF-8">
  <meta name="viewport" content="width=device-width, initial-scale=1.0">
  <title>Sample HTML5 Document</title>
 </head>
 <body>
 <header>
  <h1>Welcome to My HTML5 Page</h1>
 </header>
 <main>
  <section>
   <h2>Introduction</h2>
   <p>This is a simple HTML5 document structure example.</p>
  </section>
  <section>
   <h2>Content</h2>
   <p>HTML5 makes web development easier with its new features.</p>
  </section>
 </main>
 <footer>
  <p>&copy; 2024 Tukaram Bhagat</p>
 </footer>
 </body>
</html>
```

This document structure provides a clear and organized way to build web pages, making it easier to develop and maintain web content.

Q. 1: Which of the following is a popular text editor for web development?

  a) Microsoft Word

  b) Notepad++

  c) Excel

  d) PowerPoint

  Answer: b) Notepad++

Q. 2: Which text editor is specifically designed for coding and offers features like syntax highlighting and code completion?

  a) Visual Studio Code

  b) WordPad

  c) Adobe Reader

  d) Photoshop

  Answer: a) Visual Studio Code

Q. 3: Visual Studio Code is developed by:

  a) Apple

  b) Google

  c) Microsoft

  d) Mozilla

  Answer: c) Microsoft

Q. 4: In Sublime Text, which shortcut is used to open the command palette?

  a) Ctrl + P

  b) Ctrl + Shift + P

  c) Ctrl + F

  d) Ctrl + S

Answer: b) Ctrl + Shift + P

Q. 5: Which feature of text editors helps in identifying matching opening and closing tags?

a) Code folding

b) Syntax highlighting

c) Bracket matching

d) Auto-completion

Answer: c) Bracket matching

Q. 6: Which of the following is a popular local server software for Windows?

a) Apache HTTP Server

b) Nginx

c) XAMPP

d) Microsoft IIS

Answer: c) XAMPP

Q. 7: What does WAMP stand for?

a) Web Application Module Package

b) Windows, Apache, MySQL, PHP

c) Windows Advanced Management Program

d) Web Access Management Protocol

Answer: b) Windows, Apache, MySQL, PHP

Q. 8: Which command is used to start the local server in Node.js?

a) node server.js

b) start server

c) run server

d) npm start

Answer: a) node server.js

Q. 9: Which port is typically used by a local web server to serve web pages?

a) 21

b) 25

c) 80

d) 443

Answer: c) 80

Q. 10: Which configuration file is commonly used to set up an Apache server?

a) httpd.conf

b) apache.conf

c) server.conf

d) web.conf

Answer: a) httpd.conf

Q. 11: What is the correct doctype declaration for an HTML5 document?

a) <!DOCTYPE html>

b) <!DOCTYPE HTML5>

c) <!DOCTYPE HTML PUBLIC "-//W3C//DTD HTML 5.0//EN">

d) <!DOCTYPE HTML SYSTEM "html5.dtd">

Answer: a) <!DOCTYPE html>

Q. 12: Which tag is used to define the metadata of an HTML5 document?

a) <meta>

b) <link>

c) <script>

d) <style>

Answer: a) <meta>

Q. 13: The `<head>` section of an HTML5 document typically contains:

a) Visible content of the webpage

b) Metadata, title, links to stylesheets, and scripts

c) The main content of the document

d) Footer information

Answer: b) Metadata, title, links to stylesheets, and scripts

Q. 14: Which tag contains the main content of an HTML5 document?

a) <head>

b) <footer>

c) <body>

d) <title>

Answer: c) <body>

Q. 15: What is the purpose of the `<title>` tag in an HTML5 document?

a) To define the main heading of the webpage

b) To set the title of the document that appears in the browser tab

c) To link to external stylesheets

d) To include metadata

Answer: b) To set the title of the document that appears in the browser tab

Q. 16: Which HTML5 element is used to create a navigation link section?

a) <nav>

b) <link>

c) <menu>

d) <footer>

Answer: a) <nav>

Q. 17: The `<section>` element in HTML5 is used to:

a) Define a section in a document

b) Create a hyperlink

c) Embed multimedia

d) Add metadata

Answer: a) Define a section in a document

Q. 18: Which tag is used to specify a footer for a document or section?

a) <bottom>

b) <footer>

c) <base>

d) <section>

Answer: b) <footer>

Q. 19: Which attribute in the `<html>` tag is used to specify the language of the document?

a) lang

b) dir

c) charset

d) type

Answer: a) lang

Q. 20: In an HTML5 document, which element is used to embed an image?

a) <pic>

b) <figure>

c) <img>

d) <image>

Answer: c) <img>

3. HTML5 Document Structure

✓ Doctype Declaration
✓ Basic HTML5 Tags: `<html>`, `<head>`, `<body>`
✓ Metadata Elements: `<title>`, `<meta>`, `<link>`, `<style>`

Doctype Declaration

The **<!DOCTYPE html>** declaration is the first line of an HTML5 document. It informs the web browser that the document is written in HTML5 and should be rendered using the HTML5 standard. This declaration is crucial for ensuring that the browser interprets the HTML code correctly and displays the web page as intended.

Syntax:

```
<!DOCTYPE html>
```

Example:

```
<!DOCTYPE html>
<html lang="en">
 <head>
   <meta charset="UTF-8">
   <meta name="viewport" content="width=device-width, initial-scale=1.0">
   <title>My HTML5 Page</title>
 </head>
 <body>
   <h1>Hello, World!</h1>
 </body>
</html>
```

The **<!DOCTYPE html>** declaration must be placed at the very top of the document, before the **<html>** tag.

Basic HTML5 Tags: <html>, <head>, <body>

<html> Tag:

The **<html>** tag is the root element of an HTML document. It encloses all other HTML elements and attributes. The **lang** attribute specifies the language of the document, which helps with accessibility and search engine optimization.

Syntax:

```
<html lang="en">
```

Example:

```
<html lang="en">
  <head>
    <title>Document Title</title>
  </head>
  <body>
    <h1>Main Heading</h1>
    <p>This is a paragraph.</p>
  </body>
</html>
```

<head> Tag:

The **<head>** tag contains meta-information about the document, such as the title, character encoding, and links to external resources like stylesheets and scripts. This section does not display content directly on the web page but provides essential information for browsers and search engines.

Syntax:

```
<head>
  <meta charset="UTF-8">
  <meta name="viewport" content="width=device-width, initial-scale=1.0">
  <title>Document Title</title>
</head>
```

Example:

```
<head>
  <meta charset="UTF-8">
  <meta name="viewport" content="width=device-width, initial-scale=1.0">
  <title>My HTML5 Page</title>
  <link rel="stylesheet" href="styles.css">
</head>
```

<body> Tag:

The **<body>** tag contains the visible content of the web page. This is where all the elements that users see and interact with, such as headings, paragraphs, images, and links, are placed.

Syntax:

```
<body>
<!-- Page content goes here -->
</body>
```

Example:

```
<body>
<header>
  <h1>Welcome to My Website</h1>
</header>
<main>
  <section>
    <h2>About Us</h2>
    <p>We are a team of web developers.</p>
  </section>
</main>
<footer>
  <p>&copy; 2024 My Website</p>
</footer>
</body>
```

Metadata Elements: `<title>`, `<meta>`, `<link>`, `<style>`

<title> Tag:

The **<title>** tag defines the title of the HTML document. It appears in the browser's title bar or tab and is crucial for search engine optimization. It should be placed within the **<head>** section.

Syntax:

```
<title>Document Title</title>
```

Example:

```
<head>
 <title>My HTML5 Page</title>
</head>
```

<meta> Tag:

The **<meta>** tag provides metadata about the HTML document, such as character encoding, author, and viewport settings. Metadata helps browsers and search engines understand and display the content properly.

Common Uses:

Character Encoding:

```
<meta charset="UTF-8">
```

Viewport Settings:

```
<meta name="viewport" content="width=device-width, initial-scale=1.0">
```

Author Information:

```
<meta name="author" content="Tukaram Bhagat">
```

Example:

```
<head>
<meta charset="UTF-8">
<meta name="viewport" content="width=device-width, initial-scale=1.0">
<meta name="description" content="A brief description of the page.">
<title>My HTML5 Page</title>
</head>
```

\<link\> Tag:

The **\<link\>** tag is used to link external resources like stylesheets to the HTML document. It is placed in the `<head>` section and is commonly used to link to CSS files.

Syntax:

```
<link rel="stylesheet" href="styles.css">
```

Example:

```
<head>
  <link rel="stylesheet" href="styles.css">
</head>
```

\<style\> Tag:

The **\<style\>** tag is used to include internal CSS styles directly within the HTML document. It is placed in the **\<head\>** section and is useful for quick styling without using external CSS files.

Syntax:

```
<style>
  body {
    font-family: Arial, sans-serif;
  }
  h1 {
    color: blue;
  }
</style>
```

Example:

```
<head>
  <style>
    body {
      font-family: Arial, sans-serif;
    }
    h1 {
      color: blue;
    }
  </style>
</head>
```

In summary, understanding the basic structure of an HTML5 document and the role of key tags helps in creating well-structured and functional web pages. The **<!DOCTYPE html>** declaration ensures proper rendering, while the **<html>, <head>,** and **<body>** tags define the overall layout and content of the page. Metadata elements like **<title>, <meta>, <link>,** and **<style>** enhance the functionality and presentation of the web content.

Q. 1. Which of the following is the correct doctype declaration for an HTML5 document?

a) <!DOCTYPE html>

b) <!DOCTYPE HTML5>

c) <!DOCTYPE html5>

d) <!DOCTYPE HTML PUBLIC "-//W3C//DTD HTML 4.01//EN" "http://www.w3.org/TR/html4/strict.dtd">

Answer: a) <!DOCTYPE html>

Q. 2. Which tag is used to contain the metadata and links to scripts and stylesheets in an HTML5 document?

a) <html>

b) <head>

c) <body>

d) <meta>

Answer: b) <head>

Q. 3. Which HTML5 tag represents the root of an HTML document?

a) <head>

b) <body>

c) <html>

d) <meta>

Answer: c) <html>

Q. 4. Where should the <title> tag be placed within an HTML5 document?

a) Inside the <body> tag

b) Inside the <head> tag

c) Outside the <html> tag

d) Inside the <meta> tag

Answer: b) Inside the <head> tag

Q. 5. Which HTML5 tag is used to include external CSS files?

a) <style>

b) <link>

c) <meta>

d) <script>

Answer: b) <link>

Q. 6. What is the purpose of the <meta> tag in HTML5?

a) To define a division or section in an HTML document

b) To specify metadata about an HTML document, such as character set, author, and viewport settings

c) To link to external stylesheets

d) To create a clickable button

Answer: b) To specify metadata about an HTML document, such as character set, author, and viewport settings

Q. 7. Which of the following tags should be placed inside the <head> section of an HTML5 document?

a) <title>

b) <meta>

c) <link>

d) All of the above

Answer: d) All of the above

Q. 8. Which HTML5 tag is used to define the main content of an HTML document?

a) <html>

b) <head>

c) <body>

d) <meta>

Answer: c) <body>

Q. 9. Which attribute in the <meta> tag is used to define the character set of an HTML document?

a) charset

b) name

c) content

d) http-equiv

Answer: a) charset

Q. 10. Which HTML5 tag is used to include internal CSS within an HTML document?

a) <style>

b) <link>

c) <script>

d) <meta>

Answer: a) <style>

4. Text Formatting and Semantics

✓ Headings and Paragraphs: <h1> to <h6>, <p>
✓ Emphasis and Importance: <em>, <strong>
✓ Inline vs Block Elements
✓ Semantic HTML5 Tags: <header>, <footer>, <article>, <section>, <aside>, <nav>

Headings and Paragraphs: <h1> to <h6>, <p>

Headings: <h1> to <h6>

Headings are used to structure content hierarchically. HTML5 provides six levels of headings, from **<h1> to <h6>**, each representing a different level of importance and size. **<h1>** is the highest level, typically used for main headings, while **<h6>** is the lowest, used for sub-sections or less important headings.

Syntax:

```
<h1>Main Heading</h1>

<h2>Subheading</h2>

<h3>Sub-subheading</h3>

<h4>Sub-sub-subheading</h4>

<h5>Further Subheading</h5>

<h6>Least Important Heading</h6>
```

Example:

```
<h1>Introduction to HTML5</h1>

<h2>What is HTML5?</h2>

<h3>History and Evolution</h3>

<h4>Early Versions</h4>

<h5>HTML 4.0</h5>

<h6>HTML 4.01</h6>
```

Paragraphs: <p>

The **<p>** tag defines a paragraph of text. It is used to separate blocks of text and provide structure to the content. Paragraphs are automatically separated by margins, which help improve readability.

Syntax:

```
<p>This is a paragraph of text. It provides a block of content separated from other elements.</p>
```

Example:

```
<p>HTML5 introduces new elements and features that enhance the functionality of web pages. It simplifies the development process and improves user experience.</p>
```

Emphasis and Importance: <em>, <strong>

Emphasis: **<em>**

The **<em>** tag is used to emphasize text. Typically, text within **<em>** tags is rendered in italics, indicating a stronger emphasis on the content. Emphasis helps to convey tone or meaning.

Syntax:

```
<p>This is an <em>important</em> statement.</p>
```

Example:

```
 <p>HTML5 provides <em>semantic</em> elements that improve the readability of web
content.</p>
```

Importance: <strong>

The **<strong>** tag indicates that the enclosed text is of strong importance. Text within <strong> tags is usually rendered in bold, highlighting its significance. This tag is also used to emphasize the importance of the content.

Syntax:

```
<p>This is a <strong>critical</strong> piece of information.</p>
```

Example:

```
 <p>Using semantic HTML5 elements is <strong>essential</strong> for creating accessible
and maintainable web pages.</p>
```

Inline vs Block Elements

Block Elements

Block elements occupy the full width available and start on a new line. They create a **"block"** of content and include elements such as headings, paragraphs, divs, and sections. Block elements stack vertically.

Examples:

```
<h1>Main Heading</h1>
<p>This is a paragraph.</p>
<div>This is a block-level container.</div>
```

Inline Elements

Inline elements only occupy as much width as necessary and do not start on a new line. They flow along with the surrounding text. Inline elements include tags like **<span>, <a>, <em>, and <strong>**.

Examples:

```
<p>This is a <strong>bold</strong> word and this is <em>italicized</em> text.</p>
<a href="https://example.com">Visit Example</a>
```

Semantic HTML5 Tags: <header>, <footer>, <article>, <section>, <aside>, <nav>

Header: <header>

The **<header>** tag represents the introductory content or a set of navigational links. It typically contains headings, logo, or other introductory information.

Syntax:

```
<header>
 <h1>Website Title</h1>
 <p>Welcome to our website.</p>
</header>
```

Example:

```
<header>
 <h1>My Blog</h1>
 <nav>
  <ul>
   <li><a href="#home">Home</a></li>
   <li><a href="#about">About</a></li>
   <li><a href="#contact">Contact</a></li>
  </ul>
 </nav>
</header>
```

Footer: <footer>

The **<footer>** tag defines the footer for a document or section. It typically contains information like contact details, copyright notices, or related links.

Syntax:

```
<footer>
  <p>&copy; 2024 My Website. All rights reserved.</p>
</footer>
```

Example:

```
<footer>
  <p>&copy; 2024 My Blog. Designed by John Doe.</p>
  <ul>
    <li><a href="#privacy">Privacy Policy</a></li>
    <li><a href="#terms">Terms of Service</a></li>
  </ul>
</footer>
```

Article: <article>

The **<article>** tag represents a self-contained piece of content that can be distributed independently. It is suitable for blog posts, news articles, or forum posts.

Syntax:

```
<article>
  <h2>Article Title</h2>
  <p>Article content goes here...</p>
```

```
</article>
```

Example:

```
<article>
<h2>Understanding HTML5</h2>
<p>HTML5 introduces several new features that make web development easier and more efficient.</p>
</article>
```

Section: <section>

The **<section>** tag represents a thematic grouping of content, typically with a heading. It is used to organize related content into separate sections.

Syntax:

```
<section>
<h2>Section Title</h2>
<p>Content for this section...</p>
</section>
```

Example:

```
<section>
<h2>Features of HTML5</h2>
```

```
    <p>HTML5 offers new semantic elements, multimedia support, and improved form
handling.</p>

  </section>
```

Aside: <aside>

The **<aside>** tag represents content that is tangentially related to the content around it, often used for sidebars or supplementary information.

Syntax:

```
<aside>

 <h3>Related Links</h3>

 <ul>

  <li><a href="#link1">Link 1</a></li>

  <li><a href="#link2">Link 2</a></li>

 </li>

</aside>
```

Example:

```
<aside>

 <h3>About HTML5</h3>

 <p>HTML5 is the latest version of the HyperText Markup Language.</p>

</aside>
```

Nav: \<nav\>

The **\<nav\>** tag is used for navigation links. It groups a set of navigation links, providing a clear structure for navigating the website.

Syntax:

```
<nav>
 <ul>
  <li><a href="#home">Home</a></li>
  <li><a href="#services">Services</a></li>
  <li><a href="#contact">Contact</a></li>
 </ul>
</nav>
```

Example:

```
<nav>
 <ul>
  <li><a href="#home">Home</a></li>
  <li><a href="#about">About Us</a></li>
  <li><a href="#portfolio">Portfolio</a></li>
  <li><a href="#contact">Contact</a></li>
 </ul>
</nav>
```

In summary, HTML5 provides a range of elements and tags to structure and format web content effectively. Understanding the differences between headings, paragraphs, emphasis tags, and semantic HTML5 elements is crucial for creating well-organized, accessible, and meaningful web pages.

Check your progress

Q. 1. Which HTML tag is used to define the largest heading?

   a) <h6>

   b) <h3>

   c) <h1>

   d) <p>

   Answer: c) <h1>

Q. 2. Which tag is used to define a paragraph in HTML?

   a) <para>

   b) <p>

   c) <paragraph>

   d) <text>

   Answer: b) <p>

Q. 3. What is the correct HTML tag for emphasizing text?

   a) <i>

   b) <em>

   c) <b>

   d) <strong>

   Answer: b) <em>

Q. 4. Which tag is used to mark text as important, typically rendering it in bold?

   a) <b>

   b) <i>

   c) <em>

   d) <strong>

   Answer: d) <strong>

Q. 5. Which HTML tag represents a block-level element by default?

   a) <span>

   b) <div>

   c) <em>

   d) <strong>

   Answer: b) <div>

Q. 6. Which HTML tag represents an inline element by default?

   a) <div>

   b) <h1>

   c) <span>

   d) <p>

   Answer: c) <span>

Q. 7. Which of the following HTML5 tags is used to define a section that contains introductory content or navigational links?

   a) <header>

   b) <footer>

   c) <article>

   d) <aside>

   Answer: a) <header>

Q. 8. What does the <footer> tag in HTML5 represent?

   a) A section containing the main content

   b) A section at the bottom of a page or section, often containing author information, copyrights, or navigation links

   c) A sidebar containing additional content

   d) A section with navigation links

   Answer: b) A section at the bottom of a page or section, often containing author information, copyrights, or navigation links

Q. 9. Which tag should be used to define self-contained content that could be independently distributed or reused, such as a blog post?

  a) <section>

  b) <article>

  c) <aside>

  d) <nav>

  Answer: b) <article>

Q. 10. Which HTML5 tag is used to define a thematic grouping of content, typically with a heading?

  a) <header>

  b) <footer>

  c) <section>

  d) <aside>

  Answer: c) <section>

Q. 11. Which HTML5 tag represents content that is tangentially related to the content around it, often displayed as a sidebar?

  a) <header>

  b) <footer>

  c) <article>

  d) <aside>

  Answer: d) <aside>

Q. 12. Which HTML5 tag is used to define a set of navigation links?

  a) <header>

  b) <nav>

  c) <section>

  d) <footer>

Answer: b) <nav>

Q. 13. How many heading levels are there in HTML?

a) 3

b) 4

c) 5

d) 6

Answer: d) 6

Q. 14. What is the difference between inline and block elements in HTML?

a) Inline elements start on a new line, while block elements do not

b) Block elements start on a new line and take up the full width available, while inline elements do not start on a new line and only take up as much width as necessary

c) Inline elements take up the full width available, while block elements do not

d) Block elements cannot contain other elements, while inline elements can

Answer: b) Block elements start on a new line and take up the full width available, while inline elements do not start on a new line and only take up as much width as necessary

Q. 15. Which tag is used to mark text as emphasized in HTML, usually displayed in italics?

a) <i>

b) <strong>

c) <em>

d) <b>

Answer: c) <em>

5. Working with Links and Lists

✓ Creating Hyperlinks: **<a>**
✓ Lists: Ordered **<ol>**, Unordered **<ul>**, Definition **<dl>**
✓ Navigation Menus

Working with Links and Lists

Creating Hyperlinks: <a>

The **<a>** tag, also known as the anchor tag, is used to create hyperlinks that link to other web pages, files, email addresses, or locations within the same document. It is one of the most fundamental elements in HTML for navigation and linking.

Syntax:

```
<a href="URL">Link Text</a>
```

href: Specifies the destination of the link. It can be an absolute URL (e.g., **https://example.com**) or a relative URL (e.g., **page.html**).

target (optional): Specifies where to open the linked document. Common values include **_blank (new tab or window), _self (same frame), _parent, and _top.**

Examples:

1. Link to Another Web Page:

```
<a href="https://www.example.com">Visit Example</a>
```

Clicking this link will take you to `https://www.example.com`.

2. Link to a Specific Section within the Same Page:

```
<a href="#section1">Go to Section 1</a>
```

For this to work, there must be an element with the ID **section1** on the same page:

```
<h2 id="section1">Section 1</h2>
```

3. Link to an Email Address:

```
<a href="mailto:info@example.com">Send Email</a>
```

Clicking this link will open the default email client with a new email addressed to **info@example.com**.

Lists: Ordered <ol>, Unordered <ul>, Definition <dl>

Ordered Lists: <ol>

The **<ol>** tag is used to create an ordered list, where each item is numbered. This is useful for lists where the order of items is important.

Syntax:

```
<ol>
```

```
  <li>First item</li>
  <li>Second item</li>
  <li>Third item</li>
</ol>
```

Example:

```
<ol>
  <li>Preheat the oven to 375°F (190°C).</li>
  <li>Mix the flour, sugar, and eggs.</li>
  <li>Bake for 30 minutes.</li>
</ol>
```

Unordered Lists: <ul>

The **<ul>** tag creates an unordered list, where each item is marked with a bullet point. This type of list is used when the order of items is not important.

Syntax:

```
<ul>
  <li>Item one</li>
  <li>Item two</li>
  <li>Item three</li>
</ul>
```

Example:

```
<ul>
 <li>Apples</li>
 <li>Bananas</li>
 <li>Cherries</li>
</ul>
```

Definition Lists: <dl>

The **<dl>** tag is used for definition lists, which consist of terms and their descriptions. It includes the **<dt>** tag for defining terms and the **<dd>** tag for providing the description.

Syntax:

```
<dl>
 <dt>Term 1</dt>
 <dd>Description for term 1.</dd>
 <dt>Term 2</dt>
 <dd>Description for term 2.</dd>
</dl>
```

Example:

```
<dl>
  <dt>HTML</dt>
  <dd>HyperText Markup Language, the standard language for creating web pages.</dd>
  <dt>CSS</dt>
  <dd>Cascading Style Sheets, used to style HTML documents.</dd>
</dl>
```

Navigation Menus

Navigation menus help users find their way around a website. They are usually created using lists combined with links. A common approach is to use the `<nav>` tag to wrap a list of links, which helps in defining the navigation area semantically.

Syntax:

```
<nav>
  <ul>
    <li><a href="home.html">Home</a></li>
    <li><a href="about.html">About</a></li>
    <li><a href="services.html">Services</a></li>
    <li><a href="contact.html">Contact</a></li>
  </ul>
</nav>
```

Example:

```
<nav>
```

```
<ul>
  <li><a href="index.html">Home</a></li>
  <li><a href="portfolio.html">Portfolio</a></li>
  <li><a href="blog.html">Blog</a></li>
  <li><a href="contact.html">Contact</a></li>
</ul>
</nav>
```

In summary, the **<a>** tag is essential for creating hyperlinks, enabling navigation between pages or resources. Lists, including ordered, unordered, and definition lists, organize content in a clear and structured manner. Navigation menus are typically built using lists and links to help users navigate a website effectively. Understanding these elements and how to use them properly is crucial for creating well-organized and user-friendly web pages.

Check your progress

Q. 1. Which HTML tag is used to create a hyperlink?

a) <link>

b) <a>

c) <href>

d) <url>

Answer: b) <a>

Q. 2. Which attribute of the <a> tag specifies the URL of the page the link goes to?

a) src

b) link

c) href

d) url

Answer: c) href

Q. 3. What is the correct syntax for creating a hyperlink that opens in a new tab?

a) <a href="http://example.com" target="_self">Link</a>

b) <a href="http://example.com" target="_blank">Link</a>

c) <a link="http://example.com" target="_new">Link</a>

d) <a link="http://example.com" target="_tab">Link</a>

Answer: b) <a href="http://example.com" target="_blank">Link</a>

Q. 4. Which HTML tag is used to create an ordered list?

a) <ol>

b) <ul>

c) <li>

d) <dl>

Answer: a) <ol>

Q. 5. Which HTML tag is used to create an unordered list?

a) <ol>

b) <ul>

c) <li>

d) <dl>

Answer: b) <ul>

Q. 6. Which tag is used to define items in both ordered and unordered lists?

a) <item>

b) <li>

c) <dt>

d) <dd>

Answer: b) <li>

Q. 7. What tag is used to create a definition list in HTML?

a) <ol>

b) <ul>

c) <dl>

d) <li>

Answer: c) <dl>

Q. 8. In a definition list, which tag is used to define the term being described?

a) <dd>

b) <li>

c) <dt>

d) <dfn>

Answer: c) <dt>

Q. 9. In a definition list, which tag is used to describe the term?

a) <dd>

b) <li>

c) <dt>

d) <dfn>

Answer: a) <dd>

Q. 10. Which of the following elements would you use to create a navigation menu in HTML5?

a) <nav>

b) <header>

c) <footer>

d) <article>

Answer: a) <nav>

6. Images and Media

- ✓ **Inserting Images: `<img>`**
- ✓ **Image Formats and Optimization**
- ✓ **Embedding Audio and Video: `<audio>`, `<video>`**

Inserting Images: <img>

The **<img>** tag is used to embed images into an HTML document. Unlike other HTML elements, **<img>** is a self-closing tag and does not have a closing tag. The **src** attribute specifies the path to the image file, and the **alt** attribute provides alternative text that describes the image, which is important for accessibility.

Syntax:

```
<img src="path/to/image.jpg" alt="Description of the image" width="300" height="200">
```

src: Specifies the path to the image file. This can be a relative path, an absolute path, or a URL.

alt: Provides alternative text for the image, which is displayed if the image cannot be loaded and is used by screen readers for accessibility.

width and **height** (optional): Specify the dimensions of the image. These attributes can help control the size of the image on the page.

Example:

```
<img src="logo.png" alt="Company Logo" width="150" height="150">
```

This example inserts an image called **logo.png** with a width and height of **150 pixels** each. If the image cannot be loaded, the alt text "Company Logo" will be displayed.

Image Formats and Optimization

Image Formats:

1. JPEG (Joint Photographic Experts Group): Best suited for photographs and images with gradient colors. It supports millions of colors and provides good compression with minimal quality loss.

Example: photo.jpg

2. PNG (Portable Network Graphics): Ideal for images requiring transparency or images with sharp edges and text. PNG provides lossless compression, meaning it retains all the image data.

Example: image.png

3. GIF (Graphics Interchange Format): Suitable for simple graphics and animations. It supports a limited color palette (256 colors) and can be used for short, looping animations.

Example: animation.gif

4. WebP: A modern format that provides both lossy and lossless compression. WebP is designed to be more efficient than JPEG and PNG, offering smaller file sizes with high quality.

Example: graphic.webp

Optimization:

Optimizing images is crucial for improving website performance and load times. Here are some tips:

Resize Images: Ensure that images are not larger than they need to be. Use image editing software or online tools to resize images to the dimensions required by your website.

Compress Images: Use tools to compress images, reducing their file size without significantly affecting quality. Tools like TinyPNG, JPEG-Optimizer, or built-in features in image editing software can help with this.

Use the Right Format: Choose the appropriate image format based on the type of image and its requirements (e.g., JPEG for photographs, PNG for images with transparency).

Lazy Loading: Implement lazy loading to defer the loading of images until they are in the viewport. This improves initial page load times. Use the **loading="lazy"** attribute with the **<img>** tag:

```
<img src="image.jpg" alt="Description" loading="lazy">
```

Embedding Audio and Video: <audio>, <video>

Embedding Audio: <audio>

The **<audio>** tag is used to embed audio files into a web page. It supports several audio formats, such as MP3, Ogg, and WAV. The tag can include controls for playback, volume, and other features.

Syntax:

```
<audio controls>
  <source src="audio.mp3" type="audio/mpeg">
  Your browser does not support the audio element.
```

```
</audio>
```

controls: Adds playback controls like play, pause, and volume.

<source>: Specifies the path to the audio file and its format. Multiple <source> elements can be used to provide different formats for compatibility.

Example:

```
<audio controls>
  <source src="song.mp3" type="audio/mpeg">
  <source src="song.ogg" type="audio/ogg">
  Your browser does not support the audio element.
</audio>
```

This example embeds an audio file with both MP3 and OGG formats for broader browser support.

Embedding Video: <video>

The **<video>** tag allows you to embed video files on a web page. It supports various formats, including MP4, WebM, and Ogg. Like the **<audio>** tag, it can include controls for playback.

Syntax:

```
<video width="640" height="360" controls>
  <source src="video.mp4" type="video/mp4">
```

```
  <source src="video.webm" type="video/webm">

  Your browser does not support the video tag.

  </video>
```

width and **height**: Specify the dimensions of the video player.

controls: Adds playback controls for the user to play, pause, and adjust volume.

<source>: Specifies the path to the video file and its format. Multiple `<source>` elements can be included for different formats.

Example:

```
<video width="800" height="450" controls>

<source src="movie.mp4" type="video/mp4">

<source src="movie.webm" type="video/webm">

Your browser does not support the video tag.

</video>
```

This example embeds a video with MP4 and WebM formats, providing a fallback for browsers that may not support one of the formats.

In summary, the **<img>** tag is used for inserting images into a web page, with attributes like **src** and **alt** to specify the image source and alternative text. Understanding image formats and optimization techniques helps ensure efficient web performance. The **<audio>** and **<video>** tags enable embedding multimedia content, providing controls and support for multiple formats to enhance user experience.

Check your progress

Q. 1. Which HTML tag is used to insert an image?

a) <picture>

b) <img>

c) <src>

d) <image>

Answer: b) <img>

Q. 2. Which attribute is required in the <img> tag to specify the image file?

a) href

b) src

c) alt

d) link

Answer: b) src

Q. 3. What is the purpose of the **alt** attribute in the **<img>** tag?

a) To specify the source of the image

b) To provide alternative text if the image cannot be displayed

c) To define the height of the image

d) To link the image to another page

Answer: b) To provide alternative text if the image cannot be displayed

Q. 4. Which of the following image formats supports transparency?

a) JPEG

b) BMP

c) GIF

d) TIFF

Answer: c) GIF

Q. 5. Which image format is best known for its lossless compression and support for transparency?

a) JPEG

b) PNG

c) BMP

d) TIFF

Answer: b) PNG

Q. 6. What does the **controls** attribute do in the **<audio>** and **<video>** tags?

a) It specifies the source file for the media

b) It adds default playback controls like play, pause, and volume

c) It loops the media indefinitely

d) It defines the media's height and width

Answer: b) It adds default playback controls like play, pause, and volume

Q. 7. Which HTML tag is used to embed audio files in a webpage?

a) <sound>

b) <audio>

c) <voice>

d) <music>

Answer: b) <audio>

Q. 8. Which HTML tag is used to embed video files in a webpage?

a) <movie>

b) <video>

c) <film>

d) <clip>

Answer: b) <video>

Q. 9. Which attribute of the **<audio>** tag specifies the audio file to be played?

a) href

b) src

c) file

d) link

Answer: b) src

Q. 10. What attribute can be used in the **<audio>** and **<video>** tags to start playing the media automatically when the page loads?

a) autostart

b) autoplay

c) controls

d) play

Answer: b) autoplay

Q. 11. Which attribute in the **<video>** tag is used to specify multiple sources for the video to support different formats?

a) type

b) src

c) source

d) media

Answer: c) source

Q. 12. Which attribute would you use to loop a video continuously using the **<video>** tag?

a) replay

b) loop

c) repeat

d) cycle

Answer: b) loop

7. HTML5 Forms and Input Types

✓ Basic Form Structure: <form>, <input>, <label>
✓ New Input Types in HTML5: email, url, date, number, range
✓ Form Validation and Attributes

Basic Form Structure: <form>, <input>, <label>

The <form> Tag:

The **<form>** tag is used to create an HTML form that collects user input. It serves as a container for various form elements such as text fields, checkboxes, radio buttons, and buttons. Forms can be submitted to a server for processing using the **action** attribute, and the **method** attribute specifies how to send data (GET or POST).

Syntax:

```
<form action="submit_form.php" method="post">
<!-- Form elements go here -->
</form>
```

action: The URL where the form data will be sent for processing.

method: Defines how data should be sent. **GET** appends data to the **URL**, while **POST** sends data in the request body.

The <input> Tag:

The **<input>** tag is used to create various types of interactive fields within a form, such as text fields, checkboxes, and buttons. The type of input is determined by the **type** attribute.

Syntax:

```
<input type="text" name="username" placeholder="Enter your username">
```

type: Specifies the type of input. Common types include **text**, **password**, **checkbox**, **radio**, and **submit**.

name: The name of the input field, used to identify the form data.

placeholder: Provides a hint about the expected value of the input field.

The <label> Tag:

The **<label>** tag is used to define labels for form elements. It improves accessibility by allowing screen readers to associate the label with its corresponding input field. The **for** attribute of **<label>** should match the **id** of the associated **<input>**.

Syntax:

```
<label for="username">Username:</label>
<input type="text" id="username" name="username">
```

for: Associates the label with an input field using the input's `id`.

Example:

```
<form action="submit_form.php" method="post">
 <label for="name">Name:</label>
 <input type="text" id="name" name="name" placeholder="Enter your name">
```

```
<label for="email">Email:</label>

<input type="email" id="email" name="email" placeholder="Enter your email">


<input type="submit" value="Submit">
</form>
```

This example creates a form with text and email input fields, each paired with a label.

New Input Types in HTML5

HTML5 introduced several new input types that provide enhanced functionality and user experience. These new types help with validation and provide specific input methods suitable for different types of data.

email: Validates that the input conforms to an email address format.

Example:

```
<label for="email">Email:</label>
<input type="email" id="email" name="email" placeholder="Enter your email">
```

url: Ensures that the input is a valid URL.

Example:

```
<label for="website">Website:</label>
<input type="url" id="website" name="website" placeholder="Enter your website URL">
```

date: Provides a date picker for selecting a date.

Example:

```
<label for="birthdate">Birthdate:</label>
<input type="date" id="birthdate" name="birthdate">
```

number: Allows users to enter a numeric value and provides options for setting minimum and maximum values.

Example:

```
<label for="age">Age:</label>
<input type="number" id="age" name="age" min="0" max="120" step="1" placeholder="Enter your age">
```

range: Provides a slider to select a value within a specified range.

Example:

```
<label for="volume">Volume:</label>
<input type="range" id="volume" name="volume" min="0" max="100" value="50">
```

This creates a slider input for selecting a volume level between 0 and 100.

Form Validation and Attributes

HTML5 introduced built-in form validation features that help ensure user inputs are valid before submission. These features are controlled by various attributes that provide feedback to users and prevent incorrect data from being submitted.

required: Specifies that the input field must be filled out before the form can be submitted.

Example:

```
<label for="name">Name:</label>
<input type="text" id="name" name="name" required>
```

pattern: Defines a regular expression that the input value must match for validation.

Example:

```
<label for="phone">Phone:</label>
<input type="text" id="phone" name="phone" pattern="\d{10}" placeholder="Enter a 10-digit phone number">
```

This example validates that the input is a 10-digit number.

min and **max:** Specify the minimum and maximum values for numeric and date inputs.

Example:

```
<label for="age">Age:</label>
<input type="number" id="age" name="age" min="1" max="100">
```

step: Defines the interval between valid values for numeric inputs.

Example:

```
<label for="quantity">Quantity:</label>
<input type="number" id="quantity" name="quantity" min="1" step="5">
```

placeholder: Provides a hint or example of the expected value in the input field.

Example:

```
<label for="username">Username:</label>
<input type="text" id="username" name="username" placeholder="Enter your username">
```

disabled: Disables the input field, making it uneditable and preventing it from being included in form submissions.

Example:

```
<label for="comments">Comments:</label>

<textarea id="comments" name="comments" disabled>Comments are disabled</textarea>
```

This example shows a text area that cannot be interacted with by the user.

In summary, HTML5 forms and input types enhance user interaction and data collection by introducing new elements and attributes. The **<form>**, **<input>**, and **<label>** tags form the basis of form creation, while new input types like **email, url, date, number**, and **range** provide more precise control over user input. Form validation attributes like **required, pattern**, **min**, **max**, **step**, and **placeholder** ensure that data entered by users meets specific criteria, improving data quality and user experience.

Q. 1. Which HTML tag is used to create a form?

a) <input>

b) <label>

c) <form>

d) <fieldset>

Answer: c) <form>

Q. 2. Which attribute in the **<form>** tag specifies the URL to which the form data will be sent?

a) method

b) action

c) enctype

d) target

Answer: b) action

Q. 3. Which HTML tag is used to create a text input field in a form?

a) <input type="text">

b) <label>

c) <textarea>

d) <form>

Answer: a) <input type="text">

Q. 4. Which tag is used to associate a label with a specific form control?

a) <form>

b) <input>

c) <label>

d) <fieldset>

Answer: c) <label>

Q. 5. Which attribute in the **<input>** tag specifies that an input field must be filled out before submitting the form?

a) required

b) pattern

c) placeholder

d) value

Answer: a) required

Q. 6. What is the correct input type for accepting an email address in HTML5?

a) <input type="text">

b) <input type="email">

c) <input type="url">

d) <input type="password">

Answer: b) <input type="email">

Q. 7. Which input type is used to create a field for entering a URL in HTML5?

a) <input type="text">

b) <input type="email">

c) <input type="url">

d) <input type="search">

Answer: c) <input type="url">

Q. 8. Which input type is used to create a date picker in HTML5?

a) <input type="datetime">

b) <input type="date">

c) <input type="time">

d) <input type="month">

Answer: b) <input type="date">

Q. 9. Which input type is used to create a field for entering numbers in HTML5?

a) <input type="text">

b) <input type="number">

c) <input type="range">

d) <input type="tel">

Answer: b) <input type="number">

Q. 10. Which input type is used to create a slider control in HTML5?

a) <input type="number">

b) <input type="range">

c) <input type="slider">

d) <input type="progress">

Answer: b) <input type="range">

Q. 11. Which attribute specifies the maximum value for an **<input type="number">** field?

a) min

b) max

c) step

d) value

Answer: b) max

Q. 12. Which attribute specifies the minimum value for an **<input type="number">** field?

a) min

b) max

c) step

d) value

Answer: a) min

Q. 13. Which attribute is used to specify a default value for an input field?

a) placeholder

b) value

c) pattern

d) required

Answer: b) value

Q. 14. What does the **novalidate** attribute do when added to a **<form>** tag?

a) It disables client-side validation.

b) It disables server-side validation.

c) It makes all fields optional.

d) It submits the form data as plain text.

Answer: a) It disables client-side validation.

Q. 15. Which attribute is used to provide a regular expression for input validation?

a) required

b) pattern

c) placeholder

d) maxlength

Answer: b) pattern

Q. 16. Which input type is used to create a field for selecting a month and year in HTML5?

a) <input type="month">

b) <input type="date">

c) <input type="datetime">

d) <input type="time">

Answer: a) <input type="month">

Q. 17. Which input type is used to create a field for entering a time in HTML5?

a) <input type="datetime">`

b) <input type="date">`

c) <input type="time">`

d) <input type="month">`

Answer: c) <input type="time">`

Q. 18. Which attribute specifies that an input field should automatically get focus when the page loads?

a) required

b) placeholder

c) autofocus

d) value

Answer: c) autofocus

Q. 19. Which attribute specifies a short hint that describes the expected value of an input field?

a) required

b) placeholder

c) value

d) title

Answer: b) placeholder

Q. 20. Which input type is used for a control that lets the user select a file?

a) <input type="file">

b) <input type="text">

c) <input type="search">

d) <input type="data">

Answer: a) <input type="file">

8. Canvas and SVG

- ✓ **Drawing with the Canvas API: <canvas>**
- ✓ **Introduction to Scalable Vector Graphics (SVG)**
- ✓ **Use Cases and Examples**

Drawing with the Canvas API: <canvas>

The **<canvas>** element is an HTML5 feature that allows for dynamic, scriptable rendering of 2D shapes and bitmap images. It provides a drawing surface in a web page where graphics can be rendered using JavaScript.

Basic Syntax:

```
<canvas id="myCanvas" width="500" height="300"></canvas>
```

id: Assigns a unique identifier to the canvas element.

width and **height**: Define the dimensions of the canvas in pixels. If not specified, the default size is 300x150 pixels.

Drawing on the Canvas:

To draw on a canvas, you use JavaScript to access the canvas's 2D rendering context. Here's a basic example:

1. JavaScript Example:

```
<!DOCTYPE html>
<html lang="en">
<head>
 <meta charset="UTF-8">
 <meta name="viewport" content="width=device-width, initial-scale=1.0">
 <title>Canvas Example</title>
```

```html
  <style>
    canvas {
      border: 1px solid black;
    }
  </style>
</head>
<body>
  <canvas id="myCanvas" width="500" height="300"></canvas>
  <script>
    const canvas = document.getElementById('myCanvas');
    const ctx = canvas.getContext('2d');

    // Draw a rectangle
    ctx.fillStyle = 'blue';
    ctx.fillRect(50, 50, 200, 100);

    // Draw a circle
    ctx.beginPath();
    ctx.arc(300, 150, 50, 0, 2 * Math.PI);
    ctx.fillStyle = 'red';
    ctx.fill();

    // Draw text
    ctx.font = '24px Arial';
    ctx.fillStyle = 'green';
    ctx.fillText('Hello Canvas!', 150, 250);
  </script>
</body>
</html>
```

In this example:

- A blue rectangle is drawn.

- A red circle is drawn.

- Text is added to the canvas.

Use Cases:

- Games: Creating game graphics and animations.

- Data Visualization: Rendering charts and graphs.

- Image Manipulation: Applying effects and filters to images.

8.2 Introduction to Scalable Vector Graphics (SVG)

SVG (Scalable Vector Graphics) is an XML-based format for describing two-dimensional vector graphics. Unlike raster images (e.g., JPEG, PNG), SVG graphics are resolution-independent and can be scaled without loss of quality.

Basic Syntax:

```
<svg width="200" height="200" xmlns="http://www.w3.org/2000/svg">
  <!-- SVG content goes here -->
</svg>
```

width and height: Define the dimensions of the SVG canvas.

xmlns: Defines the XML namespace for SVG, required for proper rendering.

Basic SVG Shapes:

1. Rectangle:

```
<svg width="200" height="200">
  <rect x="10" y="10" width="100" height="50" fill="blue" />
</svg>
```

This example draws a blue rectangle positioned 10 pixels from the top and left of the SVG canvas.

2. Circle:

```
<svg width="200" height="200">
  <circle cx="100" cy="100" r="50" fill="red" />
</svg>
```

This example draws a red circle with a center at (100, 100) and a radius of 50 pixels.

3. Line:

```
<svg width="200" height="200">
  <line x1="10" y1="10" x2="150" y2="150" stroke="black" stroke-width="2" />
</svg>
```

This example draws a black line from coordinates (10, 10) to (150, 150).

Use Cases:

Icons and Logos: Creating sharp, scalable graphics for icons and branding.

Interactive Graphics: Building interactive elements such as maps and diagrams.

Data Visualization: Creating scalable charts and graphs.

Use Cases and Examples

Canvas Use Cases:

1. Game Development:

The **<canvas>** element is often used in web-based games to render game graphics, such as characters, backgrounds, and animations.

```html
<canvas id="gameCanvas" width="800" height="600"></canvas>
<script>
  const gameCanvas = document.getElementById('gameCanvas');
  const gameCtx = gameCanvas.getContext('2d');

  // Example: Draw a simple game character (circle)
  gameCtx.fillStyle = 'green';
  gameCtx.beginPath();
  gameCtx.arc(400, 300, 20, 0, 2 * Math.PI);
  gameCtx.fill();
</script>
```

2. Data Visualization:

Canvas can be used to create dynamic charts and graphs.

```html
<canvas id="chartCanvas" width="500" height="300"></canvas>
<script>
```

```javascript
const chartCanvas = document.getElementById('chartCanvas');
const chartCtx = chartCanvas.getContext('2d');


// Example: Draw a simple bar chart
chartCtx.fillStyle = 'blue';
chartCtx.fillRect(50, 250, 50, -150);
chartCtx.fillRect(120, 250, 50, -100);
chartCtx.fillRect(190, 250, 50, -200);
</script>
```

SVG Use Cases:

1. Interactive Infographics:

SVG is ideal for creating interactive infographics that can respond to user actions.

```html
<svg width="500" height="500">
  <circle cx="250" cy="250" r="100" fill="blue" />
  <text x="250" y="250" text-anchor="middle" stroke="#51c5cf" stroke-width="1px" dy=".3em">SVG Circle</text>
</svg>
```

2. Responsive Web Design:

SVG graphics scale seamlessly, making them perfect for responsive web design.

```
<svg width="100%" height="auto" viewBox="0 0 200 200">

 <rect x="10" y="10" width="180" height="180" fill="green" />

</svg>
```

This SVG will scale to fit its container while maintaining its aspect ratio.

In summary, HTML5's **<canvas>** element provides a powerful way to draw and manipulate graphics dynamically using JavaScript, suitable for applications like games and data visualization. SVG, on the other hand, offers scalable vector graphics for creating high-quality, resolution-independent images, ideal for icons, interactive graphics, and responsive web design. Both technologies enhance web development capabilities by providing versatile tools for graphical content.

Q. 1. Which HTML tag is used to draw graphics via scripting (usually JavaScript)?

- a) `<graphic>`

- b) `<canvas>`

- c) `<svg>`

- d) `<draw>`

- Answer: b) `<canvas>`

Q. 2. What attribute specifies the width of a `<canvas>` element?

- a) `style`

- b) `width`

- c) `size`

- d) `height`

- Answer: b) `width`

Q. 3. What attribute specifies the height of a `<canvas>` element?

- a) `style`

- b) `height`

- c) `size`

- d) `width`

- Answer: b) `height`

Q. 4. Which method is used to draw a rectangle on a `<canvas>`?

- a) `drawRect()`

- b) `createRect()`

- c) `fillRect()`

- d) `makeRect()`

- Answer: c) `fillRect()`

Q. 5. Which method is used to clear a specific area on a `<canvas>`?

   - a) `clearRect()`

   - b) `eraseRect()`

   - c) `removeRect()`

   - d) `deleteRect()`

   - Answer: a) `clearRect()`

Q. 6. Which HTML tag is used to define Scalable Vector Graphics?

   - a) `<canvas>`

   - b) `<svg>`

   - c) `<vector>`

   - d) `<draw>`

   - Answer: b) `<svg>`

Q. 7. Which SVG element is used to draw a circle?

   - a) `<circle>`

   - b) `<ellipse>`

   - c) `<round>`

   - d) `<path>`

   - Answer: a) `<circle>`

Q. 8. Which SVG element is used to draw a rectangle?

   - a) `<rect>`

   - b) `<square>`

   - c) `<box>`

   - d) `<shape>`

   - Answer: a) `<rect>`

Q. 9. What attribute of the `<circle>` element defines the radius of the circle in SVG?

  - a) `r`

  - b) `radius`

  - c) `size`

  - d) `length`

  - Answer: a) `r`

Q. 10. Which attribute is used to set the color of an SVG shape's stroke?

  - a) `fill`

  - b) `color`

  - c) `stroke`

  - d) `line`

  - Answer: c) `stroke`

Q. 11. What is the primary difference between `<canvas>` and `<svg>`?

  - a) `<canvas>` uses XML to define graphics, `<svg>` uses JavaScript

  - b) `<canvas>` is resolution independent, `<svg>` is resolution dependent

  - c) `<canvas>` is resolution dependent, `<svg>` is resolution independent

  - d) `<canvas>` and `<svg>` have no significant differences

  - Answer: c) `<canvas>` is resolution dependent, `<svg>` is resolution independent

Q. 12. Which method is used to draw a path in `<canvas>`?

  - a) `drawPath()`

  - b) `beginPath()`

  - c) `createPath()`

  - d) `makePath()`

  - Answer: b) `beginPath()`

Q. 13. Which SVG element is used to draw text?

- a) `<text>`

- b) `<label>`

- c) `<caption>`

- d) `<font>`

- Answer: a) `<text>`

Q. 14. In SVG, which attribute is used to define the font size of the text?

- a) `size`

- b) `font-size`

- c) `text-size`

- d) `font`

- Answer: b) `font-size`

Q. 15. Which method is used to draw an image onto a `<canvas>`?

- a) `drawImage()`

- b) `createImage()`

- c) `fillImage()`

- d) `makeImage()`

- Answer: a) `drawImage()`

9. Geolocation API

- ✓ **Understanding Geolocation**
- ✓ **Implementing Geolocation in Web Pages**
- ✓ **Privacy and Security Considerations**

Geolocation API

The Geolocation API allows web applications to access the geographical location of a user's device. This can be used for various purposes, such as location-based services, personalized content, and user-specific functionalities.

Understanding Geolocation

Geolocation involves determining the physical location of a device. This can be achieved using different methods, each providing varying degrees of accuracy:

GPS (Global Positioning System): Uses satellite signals to provide precise location data. It's commonly used in mobile devices and outdoor navigation systems.

IP Address: Estimates location based on the IP address assigned by the internet service provider. This method provides approximate location information and is less accurate than GPS.

Wi-Fi and Cell Tower Triangulation: Determines location by measuring the signal strength from nearby Wi-Fi networks or cell towers. This method is often used in urban environments where GPS signals may be weak.

Geolocation Data Example:

```json
{
  "coords": {
    "latitude": 37.7749,
    "longitude": -122.4194,
    "altitude": 0,
    "accuracy": 10,
    "altitudeAccuracy": null,
```

```
  "heading": null,

  "speed": null

},

  "timestamp": 1633043073414

}
```

In this example, `latitude` and `longitude` represent the geographical coordinates, while `accuracy` indicates the precision of the location data in meters.

Implementing Geolocation in Web Pages

To use the Geolocation API in web pages, you access the **navigator.geolocation** object provided by the browser. This API includes methods for retrieving location data and handling errors.

Basic Implementation:

1. Getting the Current Position:

Use the **getCurrentPosition()** method to retrieve the user's current location. This method requires a success callback function and optionally an error callback function.

```
<!DOCTYPE html>

<html lang="en">

<head>

 <meta charset="UTF-8">

 <meta name="viewport" content="width=device-width, initial-scale=1.0">

 <title>Geolocation Example</title>
```

```html
</head>
<body>
 <button onclick="getLocation()">Get Location</button>
 <p id="location"></p>

 <script>
  function getLocation() {
   if (navigator.geolocation) {
    navigator.geolocation.getCurrentPosition(showPosition, showError);
   } else {
    document.getElementById('location').innerHTML = "Geolocation is not supported by this browser.";
   }
  }

  function showPosition(position) {
   const latitude = position.coords.latitude;
   const longitude = position.coords.longitude;
   document.getElementById('location').innerHTML =
    `Latitude: ${latitude}<br>Longitude: ${longitude}`;
  }

  function showError(error) {
   switch (error.code) {
    case error.PERMISSION_DENIED:
     document.getElementById('location').innerHTML = "User denied the request for Geolocation.";
     break;
    case error.POSITION_UNAVAILABLE:
```

```
        document.getElementById('location').innerHTML  =  "Location  information  is
unavailable.";

      break;

    case error.TIMEOUT:

        document.getElementById('location').innerHTML = "The request to get user location
timed out.";

      break;

    case error.UNKNOWN_ERROR:

        document.getElementById('location').innerHTML = "An unknown error occurred.";

      break;

    }

  }

  </script>

  </body>

  </html>
```

In this example:

Clicking the **"Get Location"** button triggers the **getLocation()** function.

The **showPosition()** function displays the latitude and longitude.

The **showError()** function handles any errors that occur.

2. Watch Position:

Use the **watchPosition()** method to continuously monitor the user's position. This method returns an ID that can be used to stop monitoring with **clearWatch()**.

```html
<!DOCTYPE html>
<html lang="en">
<head>
 <meta charset="UTF-8">
 <meta name="viewport" content="width=device-width, initial-scale=1.0">
 <title>Watch Position Example</title>
</head>
<body>
 <button onclick="startWatching()">Start Watching</button>
 <button onclick="stopWatching()">Stop Watching</button>
 <p id="watchLocation"></p>

 <script>
  let watchId;

  function startWatching() {
   if (navigator.geolocation) {
    watchId = navigator.geolocation.watchPosition(showPosition, showError);
   } else {
    document.getElementById('watchLocation').innerHTML = "Geolocation is not supported by this browser.";
   }
  }

  function stopWatching() {
   if (navigator.geolocation && watchId) {
    navigator.geolocation.clearWatch(watchId);
    document.getElementById('watchLocation').innerHTML = "Stopped watching position.";
```

```javascript
  }

 }


 function showPosition(position) {

  const latitude = position.coords.latitude;

  const longitude = position.coords.longitude;

  document.getElementById('watchLocation').innerHTML =

   `Latitude: ${latitude}<br>Longitude: ${longitude}`;

 }


 function showError(error) {

  switch (error.code) {

   case error.PERMISSION_DENIED:

    document.getElementById('watchLocation').innerHTML = "User denied the request
for Geolocation.";

    break;

   case error.POSITION_UNAVAILABLE:

    document.getElementById('watchLocation').innerHTML = "Location information is
unavailable.";

    break;

   case error.TIMEOUT:

    document.getElementById('watchLocation').innerHTML = "The request to get user
location timed out.";

    break;

   case error.UNKNOWN_ERROR:

    document.getElementById('watchLocation').innerHTML = "An unknown error
occurred.";

    break;

  }

 }
```

```
    </script>

</body>

</html>
```

In this example:

- The **"Start Watching"** button begins to monitor the user's location.

- The **"Stop Watching"** button stops the monitoring.

Privacy and Security Considerations

When implementing the Geolocation API, it is important to consider privacy and security implications:

1. User Consent:

Browsers require user permission to access location data. Always prompt the user to allow or deny access and respect their choice.

Provide a clear explanation of why location data is needed and how it will be used.

2. Data Protection:

Ensure that location data is handled securely. Avoid storing or transmitting sensitive location information unless necessary.

Use HTTPS to encrypt data transmitted between the client and server.

3. Accuracy and Use:

Be aware of the accuracy of the location data. Different methods provide varying levels of precision, and the data may not always be accurate.

Only request location data when it is essential for the application's functionality.

4. Ethical Use:

Avoid using location data in ways that could compromise user privacy or be perceived as invasive.

Ensure that location-based features align with ethical guidelines and legal requirements.

Example of Handling Privacy:

```html
<!DOCTYPE html>
<html lang="en">
<head>
  <meta charset="UTF-8">
  <meta name="viewport" content="width=device-width, initial-scale=1.0">
  <title>Privacy Notice</title>
</head>
<body>
  <button onclick="getLocation()">Get Location</button>
  <p id="privacyNotice"></p>

  <script>
    function getLocation() {
      if (navigator.geolocation) {
        // Display a notice about why location data is needed
        document.getElementById('privacyNotice').innerHTML =
          "We need your location to provide local weather updates. Your location data will not be stored or shared.";

        navigator.geolocation.getCurrentPosition(showPosition, showError);
      } else {
```

```javascript
      document.getElementById('privacyNotice').innerHTML = "Geolocation is not supported
by this browser.";

    }

  }


  function showPosition(position) {

    const latitude = position.coords.latitude;

    const longitude = position.coords.longitude;

    document.getElementById('privacyNotice').innerHTML =

      `Latitude: ${latitude}<br>Longitude: ${longitude}`;

  }


  function showError(error) {

    switch (error.code) {

      case error.PERMISSION_DENIED:

        document.getElementById('privacyNotice').innerHTML = "User denied the request for
Geolocation.";

        break;

      case error.POSITION_UNAVAILABLE:

        document.getElementById('privacyNotice').innerHTML = "Location information is
unavailable.";

        break;

      case error.TIMEOUT:

        document.getElementById('privacyNotice').innerHTML = "The request to get user
location timed out.";

        break;

      case error.UNKNOWN_ERROR:

        document.getElementById('privacyNotice').innerHTML = "An unknown error
occurred.";

        break;

    }
```

```
    }
  </script>
</body>
</html>
```

In this example, a privacy notice is displayed before accessing the user's location, explaining why the data is needed and ensuring transparency.

In summary, the Geolocation API provides a method to access a user's location for enhancing web applications. Proper implementation involves understanding how geolocation works, implementing the API effectively, and addressing privacy and security considerations to maintain user trust and comply with best practices.

Q. 1. What does the Geolocation API provide?

a) The ability to store local data on the user's device

b) The ability to access and manipulate the user's geographical location

c) The ability to create 3D graphics on the web

d) The ability to enhance the performance of web applications

Answer: b) The ability to access and manipulate the user's geographical location

Q. 2. Which method is used to get the current position of the user in the Geolocation API?

a) getPosition()

b) getCurrentPosition()

c) watchPosition()

d) currentPosition()

Answer: b) getCurrentPosition()

Q. 3. Which method is used to continually monitor the position of the user?

a) getCurrentPosition()

b) trackPosition()

c) watchPosition()

d) monitorPosition()

Answer: c) watchPosition()

Q. 4. What method is used to stop watching the user's position?

a) stopPosition()

b) clearPosition()

c) stopWatchPosition()

d) clearWatch()

Answer: d) clearWatch()

Q. 5. Which object contains the geographical coordinates returned by the **Geolocation** API?

    a) Coordinates

    b) GeolocationCoordinates

    c) Position

    d) GeoPosition

    Answer: a) Coordinates

Q. 6. What are the three main properties of the **Coordinates** object?

    a) latitude, longitude, altitude

    b) latitude, longitude, accuracy

    c) latitude, longitude, speed

    d) latitude, longitude, heading

    Answer: b) latitude, longitude, accuracy

Q. 7. What is a key privacy consideration when using the Geolocation API?

    a) Geolocation data is not shared with the server

    b) Users must always be notified and give consent before their location is accessed

    c) Geolocation data is stored indefinitely on the client side

    d) Geolocation data is automatically encrypted

    Answer: b) Users must always be notified and give consent before their location is accessed

Q. 8. Which error code in the Geolocation API indicates that the user has denied permission for location access?

    a) 1

    b) 2

    c) 3

    d) 4

    Answer: a) 1

Q. 9. Which parameter of the **getCurrentPosition** method is optional and allows developers to customize the behavior of the Geolocation API?

a) options

b) settings

c) config

d) preferences

Answer: a) options

Q. 10. What is the purpose of the **enableHighAccuracy** option in the Geolocation API?

a) To ensure the location data is retrieved faster

b) To allow the application to use GPS for more precise location data

c) To increase the accuracy of the position returned by the API at the expense of slower response time

d) To use network-based geolocation services

Answer: c) To increase the accuracy of the position returned by the API at the expense of slower response time

10. Web Storage

- ✓ **Local Storage vs. Session Storage**
- ✓ **Using the Web Storage API**
- ✓ **Storing and Retrieving Data**

Web Storage

Web Storage is a web API that provides a way to store data on the client side, which can be used to enhance user experiences by persisting data across page reloads and sessions. It is part of HTML5 and includes two main types of storage: Local Storage and Session Storage.

Local Storage vs. Session Storage

Local Storage and Session Storage are two types of web storage that allow websites to store data in the browser. They differ in their persistence and scope:

1. Local Storage:

Persistence: Data stored in Local Storage persists even after the browser is closed and reopened. It remains available until explicitly deleted by the user or the application.

Scope: Data is stored domain-specific, meaning it is accessible only from the same domain that stored it.

Use Case: Ideal for storing data that should be retained across multiple sessions, such as user preferences or settings.

Example:

```javascript
// Storing data in Local Storage
localStorage.setItem('username', 'JohnDoe');


// Retrieving data from Local Storage
const username = localStorage.getItem('username');
console.log(username); // Output: JohnDoe
```

```
// Removing data from Local Storage

localStorage.removeItem('username');


// Clearing all data from Local Storage

localStorage.clear();
```

2. Session Storage:

Persistence: Data stored in Session Storage is available only for the duration of the page session. It is cleared when the page session ends, which typically happens when the browser tab is closed.

Scope: Similar to Local Storage, data is domain-specific, but only available in the tab or window where it was stored.

Use Case: Suitable for storing data that should only be kept for the duration of a page session, such as form data or temporary user input.

Example:

```
// Storing data in Session Storage

sessionStorage.setItem('sessionToken', 'abc123');


// Retrieving data from Session Storage

const sessionToken = sessionStorage.getItem('sessionToken');

console.log(sessionToken); // Output: abc123
```

```
// Removing data from Session Storage

sessionStorage.removeItem('sessionToken');


// Clearing all data from Session Storage

sessionStorage.clear();
```

Using the Web Storage API

The Web Storage API provides methods for interacting with Local Storage and Session Storage. These methods allow you to store, retrieve, update, and delete data in a straightforward manner.

Web Storage API Methods:

setItem(key, value)`: Stores a value associated with a key.

getItem(key): Retrieves the value associated with a key.

removeItem(key): Removes the value associated with a key.

clear(): Clears all key-value pairs from storage.

key(index): Retrieves the key at a specific index.

Example of Using the Web Storage API:

```
<!DOCTYPE html>
<html lang="en">
<head>
 <meta charset="UTF-8">
 <meta name="viewport" content="width=device-width, initial-scale=1.0">
 <title>Web Storage Example</title>
```

```html
</head>
<body>
 <h1>Web Storage Example</h1>
 <input type="text" id="dataInput" placeholder="Enter data">
 <button onclick="storeData()">Store Data</button>
 <button onclick="retrieveData()">Retrieve Data</button>
 <button onclick="clearData()">Clear Data</button>
 <p id="output"></p>

 <script>
  function storeData() {
    const data = document.getElementById('dataInput').value;
    localStorage.setItem('myData', data);
    document.getElementById('output').innerHTML = 'Data stored!';
  }

  function retrieveData() {
    const data = localStorage.getItem('myData');
    document.getElementById('output').innerHTML = data ? `Stored Data: ${data}` : 'No data found.';
  }

  function clearData() {
    localStorage.removeItem('myData');
    document.getElementById('output').innerHTML = 'Data cleared!';
  }
 </script>
</body>
</html>
```

In this example:

storeData() stores the value from an input field into Local Storage under the key **myData**.

retrieveData() retrieves and displays the stored data.

clearData() removes the stored data.

Storing and Retrieving Data

Storing and retrieving data using the Web Storage API is straightforward. Here's a detailed explanation of how to handle data with both Local Storage and Session Storage:

1. Storing Data:

To store data, use the **setItem()** method, which requires a key and a value. The key is used to identify the data, while the value is the data itself.

```
 // Store a string in Local Storage

localStorage.setItem('userName', 'Alice');


// Store an object in Local Storage (converted to JSON)

const user = { name: 'Bob', age: 30 };

localStorage.setItem('user', JSON.stringify(user));


To store data in Session Storage, use a similar approach:


// Store a string in Session Storage

sessionStorage.setItem('sessionID', 'xyz456');
```

```
// Store an object in Session Storage (converted to JSON)

const sessionData = { token: 'abc123', expires: '2024-12-31' };

sessionStorage.setItem('sessionData', JSON.stringify(sessionData));
```

2. Retrieving Data:

To retrieve data, use the **getItem()** method with the key used for storage. For objects stored as JSON, parse the JSON string to convert it back to an object.

```
// Retrieve a string from Local Storage

const userName = localStorage.getItem('userName');

console.log(userName); // Output: Alice


// Retrieve and parse an object from Local Storage

const user = JSON.parse(localStorage.getItem('user'));

console.log(user.name); // Output: Bob
```

For Session Storage:

```
// Retrieve a string from Session Storage

const sessionID = sessionStorage.getItem('sessionID');

console.log(sessionID); // Output: xyz456
```

```
// Retrieve and parse an object from Session Storage

const sessionData = JSON.parse(sessionStorage.getItem('sessionData'));

console.log(sessionData.token); // Output: abc123
```

3. Handling Data:

Update Data: To update existing data, simply use **setItem()** with the same key. The new value will overwrite the old value.

```
localStorage.setItem('userName', 'Charlie'); // Updates the stored name to Charlie
```

Delete Data: To remove a specific item, use **removeItem()** with the key.

```
localStorage.removeItem('userName'); // Deletes the stored name
```

Clear All Data: To clear all data from storage, use **clear()**.

```
localStorage.clear(); // Clears all data from Local Storage
```

List Keys: Use `key(index)` to get the key at a specific index, which can be useful for iterating over stored data.

```
const key = localStorage.key(0); // Retrieves the first key
```

```
console.log(key);
```

In summary, Web Storage provides a convenient way to store data on the client side with Local Storage and Session Storage. Understanding how to use these storage mechanisms effectively allows you to create more dynamic and user-friendly web applications.

Check your progress

Q. 1. What are the two types of Web Storage in HTML5?

  a) Cookie Storage and Cache Storage

  b) Local Storage and Session Storage

  c) Persistent Storage and Temporary Storage

  d) File Storage and Object Storage

  Answer: b) Local Storage and Session Storage

Q. 2. Which method is used to store data in Local Storage?

  a) setItem()

b) storeItem()

c) putItem()

d) saveItem()

Answer: a) setItem()

Q. 3. Which method is used to retrieve data from Local Storage?

a) getItem()

b) retrieveItem()

c) fetchItem()

d) loadItem()

Answer: a) getItem()

Q. 4. What is the primary difference between Local Storage and Session Storage?

a) Local Storage is cleared when the page session ends; Session Storage persists even after the browser is closed.

b) Local Storage persists even after the browser is closed; Session Storage is cleared when the page session ends.

c) Local Storage has a smaller storage limit than Session Storage.

d) Local Storage is more secure than Session Storage.

Answer: b) Local Storage persists even after the browser is closed; Session Storage is cleared when the page session ends.

Q. 5. How can you remove a specific item from Local Storage?

a) deleteItem()

b) clearItem()

c) removeItem()

d) eraseItem()

Answer: c) removeItem()

Q. 6. Which method is used to clear all data stored in Local Storage?

a) clearAll()

b) removeAll()

c) deleteAll()

d) clear()

Answer: d) clear()

Q. 7. What is the storage limit for Local Storage in most modern browsers?

a) 5MB

b) 10MB

c) 50MB

d) 100MB

Answer: a) 5MB

Q. 8. Which object is used to access Session Storage in JavaScript?

a) localStorage

b) sessionStorage

c) webStorage

d) browserStorage

Answer: b) sessionStorage

Q. 9. How can you store a JSON object in Local Storage?

a) localStorage.setItem('key', object)

b) localStorage.setItem('key', JSON.stringify(object))

c) localStorage.setJSON('key', object)

d) localStorage.putItem('key', object)

Answer: b) localStorage.setItem('key', JSON.stringify(object))

Q. 10. Which method is used to remove a specific item from Session Storage?

a) deleteItem()

b) clearItem()

c) removeItem()

d) eraseItem()

Answer: c) removeItem()

Q. 11. How can you check if Local Storage is supported by the browser?

a) if (window.localStorage != undefined)

b) if (window.localStorage)

c) if (typeof(Storage) !== "undefined")

d) if (typeof(localStorage) !== "undefined")

Answer: c) if (typeof(Storage) !== "undefined")

Q. 12. Which of the following is true about the data stored in Web Storage?

a) It is sent to the server with every HTTP request.

b) It is only accessible to the same domain that stored it.

c) It is automatically encrypted.

d) It can only store string data.

Answer: b) It is only accessible to the same domain that stored it.

Q. 13. Which method is used to retrieve the value associated with a key from Session Storage?

a) fetchItem()

b) getItem()

c) retrieveItem()

d) loadItem()

Answer: b) getItem()

Q. 14. What happens if you try to store a key-value pair in Local Storage that exceeds the storage limit?

a) The oldest data is automatically removed to make space.

b) The new key-value pair is not stored, and an exception is thrown.

c) The new key-value pair is stored, and the storage limit is increased.

d) The browser prompts the user to increase the storage limit.

Answer: b) The new key-value pair is not stored, and an exception is thrown.

Q. 15. Which method is used to clear all data stored in Session Storage?

a) clearAll()

b) removeAll()

c) deleteAll()

d) clear()

Answer: d) clear()

Q. 16. What is the storage limit for Session Storage in most modern browsers?

a) 5MB

b) 10MB

c) 50MB

d) 100MB

Answer: a) 5MB

Q. 17. How can you store a number in Local Storage?

a) localStorage.setItem('key', number)

b) localStorage.setItem('key', number.toString())

c) localStorage.putItem('key', number)

d) localStorage.setNumber('key', number)

Answer: b) localStorage.setItem('key', number.toString())

Q. 18. What will the method localStorage.getItem('nonexistentKey') return if the key does not exist?

a) null

b) undefined

c) "" (empty string)

d) false

Answer: a) null

Q. 19. Can you store an array in Session Storage directly?

a) Yes, by using sessionStorage.setItem('key', array)

b) No, you must first convert the array to a string using JSON.stringify()

c) Yes, by using sessionStorage.putItem('key', array)

d) No, arrays cannot be stored in Session Storage

Answer: b) No, you must first convert the array to a string using JSON.stringify()

Q. 20. Which method is used to remove all key-value pairs from Local Storage?

a) clearAll()

b) removeAll()

c) deleteAll()

d) clear()

Answer: d) clear()

11. CSS3 and HTML5

- ✓ **Styling HTML5 Elements with CSS3**
- ✓ **New CSS3 Features: Flexbox, Grid**
- ✓ **Media Queries for Responsive Design**

Enhancing HTML5 with CSS and JavaScript

HTML5 provides a robust structure for web pages, but CSS3 and JavaScript are essential for styling and adding dynamic behavior. This section explores how CSS3 and HTML5 work together, focusing on styling HTML5 elements, new CSS3 features, and responsive design with media queries.

Styling HTML5 Elements with CSS3

CSS3 (Cascading Style Sheets, level 3) is the latest version of CSS, which introduces a range of new features and enhancements for styling web pages. When combined with HTML5, CSS3 allows for sophisticated styling of web elements and improved visual presentation.

Styling HTML5 Elements:

HTML5 introduces new semantic elements such as <header>, <footer>, <article>, and <section>. These elements can be styled using CSS3 just like traditional HTML elements. CSS3 allows you to apply various styles, including colors, fonts, layout, and more.

Example:

```
<!DOCTYPE html>
<html lang="en">
<head>
 <meta charset="UTF-8">
 <meta name="viewport" content="width=device-width, initial-scale=1.0">
 <title>CSS3 and HTML5 Example</title>
 <style>
  body {
    font-family: Arial, sans-serif;
```

```css
      margin: 0;

      padding: 0;

      background-color: #f4f4f4;

    }


    header {

      background-color: #333;

      color: #fff;

      padding: 20px;

      text-align: center;

    }


    article {

      margin: 20px;

      padding: 20px;

      background-color: #fff;

      border-radius: 5px;

      box-shadow: 0 0 10px rgba(0, 0, 0, 0.1);

    }


    footer {

      background-color: #333;

      color: #fff;

      padding: 10px;

      text-align: center;

    }
  </style>
</head>
<body>
```

```
<header>
  <h1>My HTML5 Page</h1>
</header>
<article>
  <h2>Welcome to My Page</h2>
  <p>This is an example of styling HTML5 elements with CSS3.</p>
</article>
<footer>
  <p>&copy; 2024 My Website</p>
</footer>
</body>
</html>
```

In this example:

The <header>, <article>, and <footer> elements are styled using CSS3 properties such as background-color, padding, and box-shadow.

New CSS3 Features: Flexbox, Grid

CSS3 introduces several advanced layout techniques that provide more control and flexibility for designing web pages. Two notable features are Flexbox and Grid.

Flexbox (Flexible Box Layout):

Purpose: Flexbox is a layout model designed for one-dimensional layouts. It simplifies the alignment, distribution, and sizing of items within a container.

Key Properties:

- display: flex: Defines a flex container.

- flex-direction: Specifies the direction of flex items (row, column).

- justify-content: Aligns items along the main axis (e.g., center, space-between).

- align-items: Aligns items along the cross axis (e.g., center, stretch).

Example:

```html
<!DOCTYPE html>
<html lang="en">
<head>
<meta charset="UTF-8">
<meta name="viewport" content="width=device-width, initial-scale=1.0">
<title>Flexbox Example</title>
<style>
  .container {
    display: flex;
    justify-content: space-around;
    align-items: center;
    height: 100vh;
    background-color: #f4f4f4;
  }

  .box {
    width: 100px;
    height: 100px;
    background-color: #4CAF50;
```

```
      color: white;

      display: flex;

      justify-content: center;

      align-items: center;

      font-size: 20px;

      border-radius: 5px;

    }

  </style>

</head>

<body>

  <div class="container">

    <div class="box">1</div>

    <div class="box">2</div>

    <div class="box">3</div>

  </div>

</body>

</html>
```

In this example:

The **.container** uses Flexbox to align its child **.box** elements horizontally with space around them.

The **.box** elements are centered within the container using Flexbox properties.

Grid (CSS Grid Layout):

Purpose: CSS Grid is a two-dimensional layout system that allows for the creation of complex grid-based designs with ease.

Key Properties:

- display: grid: Defines a grid container.

- grid-template-columns and grid-template-rows: Defines the number and size of columns and rows.

- grid-area: Defines a grid item's position within the grid.

Example:

```html
<!DOCTYPE html>
<html lang="en">
<head>
<meta charset="UTF-8">
<meta name="viewport" content="width=device-width, initial-scale=1.0">
<title>Grid Example</title>
<style>
  .grid-container {
    display: grid;
    grid-template-columns: repeat(3, 1fr);
    grid-gap: 10px;
    padding: 10px;
    background-color: #f4f4f4;
  }

  .grid-item {
    background-color: #4CAF50;
    color: white;
    padding: 20px;
```

```
            text-align: center;

            border-radius: 5px;

            font-size: 20px;

        }

    </style>

</head>

<body>

    <div class="grid-container">

        <div class="grid-item">1</div>

        <div class="grid-item">2</div>

        <div class="grid-item">3</div>

        <div class="grid-item">4</div>

        <div class="grid-item">5</div>

        <div class="grid-item">6</div>

    </div>

</body>

</html>
```

In this example:

The **.grid-container** uses CSS Grid to create a three-column layout with evenly spaced grid items.

The `grid-gap` property adds space between the grid items.

Media Queries for Responsive Design

Media Queries are a key feature of CSS3 that enable responsive design. They allow you to apply different styles based on the characteristics of the device, such as screen size, resolution, and orientation.

Key Concepts:

Breakpoints: Define the screen sizes where your layout should change. Common breakpoints include small devices (phones), medium devices (tablets), and large devices (desktops).

Media Query Syntax:

```css
@media (condition) {
  /* CSS rules */
}
```

Example:

```html
<!DOCTYPE html>
<html lang="en">
<head>
  <meta charset="UTF-8">
  <meta name="viewport" content="width=device-width, initial-scale=1.0">
  <title>Responsive Design Example</title>
```

```
<style>
  body {
    font-family: Arial, sans-serif;
  }

  .container {
    width: 100%;
    padding: 20px;
    box-sizing: border-box;
  }

  .box {
    background-color: #4CAF50;
    color: white;
    padding: 20px;
    text-align: center;
    border-radius: 5px;
    margin: 10px 0;
  }

  /* Default styles */
  .box {
    font-size: 20px;
  }

  /* Media query for tablets */
  @media (max-width: 768px) {
    .box {
      font-size: 18px;
```

```
    padding: 15px;

  }

}


/* Media query for mobile phones */

@media (max-width: 480px) {

  .box {

    font-size: 16px;

    padding: 10px;

  }

}
</style>
</head>
<body>
 <div class="container">
  <div class="box">Responsive Box</div>
  <div class="box">Resize the window to see changes</div>
 </div>
</body>
</html>
```

In this example:

- Default styles apply to all screen sizes.

- Media queries adjust the font size and padding of `.box` based on the screen width. For tablets (max-width: 768px) and mobile phones (max-width: 480px), the font size and padding are reduced to fit smaller screens.

Summary:

Styling HTML5 Elements with CSS3: CSS3 enhances the styling of HTML5 elements with advanced properties and features, making it easier to create visually appealing and consistent designs.

New CSS3 Features: Flexbox and Grid layout systems offer powerful tools for creating responsive and complex layouts with ease.

Media Queries: Enable responsive design by applying different styles based on device characteristics, ensuring that web pages look great on all screen sizes.

By leveraging CSS3 features and media queries, you can create modern, responsive web designs that provide

Check your progress

Q. 1. Which CSS property is used to change the text color of an element?

a) font-color

b) color

c) text-color

d) background-color

Answer: b) color

Q. 2. Which CSS selector is used to target an HTML5 <article> element?

a) .article

b) #article

c) article

d) @article

Answer: c) article

Q. 3. Which CSS property is used to change the background color of an HTML element?

a) background-color

b) color

c) bg-color

d) back-color

Answer: a) background-color

4. Which CSS property is used to create a flexible box layout?

a) display: block

b) display: flex

c) display: inline-block

d) display: box

Answer: b) display: flex

5. Which CSS property is used to create a grid layout?

a) display: flex

b) display: block

c) display: grid

d) display: inline-grid

Answer: c) display: grid

Q. 6. In Flexbox, which property is used to define the space between items?

a) space-between

b) justify-content

c) align-items

d) flex-gap

Answer: b) justify-content

Q. 7. In CSS Grid, which property is used to define the number of columns in a grid layout?

　　a) grid-template-rows

　　b) grid-template-columns

　　c) grid-rows

　　d) grid-columns

　　Answer: b) grid-template-columns

Q. 8. What is the purpose of media queries in CSS3?

　　a) To create animations

　　b) To apply styles based on device characteristics

　　c) To define grid layouts

　　d) To reset default browser styles

　　Answer: b) To apply styles based on device characteristics

Q. 9. Which of the following is a correct syntax for a media query targeting screens wider than 600px?

　　a) @media screen and (max-width: 600px)

　　b) @media screen and (min-width: 600px)

　　c) @media screen only and (min-width: 600px)

　　d) @media screen only and (max-width: 600px)

　　Answer: b) @media screen and (min-width: 600px)

Q. 10. Which keyword is used in media queries to target devices with a specific aspect ratio?

　　a) aspect

　　b) aspect-ratio

　　c) ratio

　　d) device-ratio

Answer: b) aspect-ratio

12. JavaScript and HTML5

- ✓ **Integrating JavaScript with HTML5**
- ✓ **DOM Manipulation**
- ✓ **Event Handling in HTML5**

JavaScript is a powerful scripting language that enables dynamic content and interactive features on web pages. When combined with HTML5, it enhances the functionality of web applications by allowing for real-time updates, user interaction, and more. This section explores how to integrate JavaScript with HTML5, manipulate the DOM (Document Object Model), and handle events.

Integrating JavaScript with HTML5

JavaScript can be integrated with HTML5 to add interactivity and dynamic behavior to web pages. This is done by embedding JavaScript code directly within HTML documents or by linking to external JavaScript files.

1. Inline JavaScript:

You can include JavaScript code directly within an HTML document using the `<script>` tag. This is typically used for small scripts or when you want to include JavaScript code directly within an HTML page.

Example:

```html
<!DOCTYPE html>
<html lang="en">
<head>
  <meta charset="UTF-8">
  <meta name="viewport" content="width=device-width, initial-scale=1.0">
  <title>Inline JavaScript Example</title>
</head>
<body>
  <h1>Hello, JavaScript!</h1>
  <button onclick="showMessage()">Click Me</button>
```

```
<script>
  function showMessage() {
    alert('Button was clicked!');
  }
</script>
</body>
</html>
```

In this example:

- The `<script>` tag contains JavaScript code that defines the `showMessage()` function.

- The `onclick` attribute of the `<button>` element calls this function when the button is clicked.

2. External JavaScript:

For larger scripts or to keep HTML and JavaScript code separate, you can use external JavaScript files. Link to these files using the `<script>` tag with the `src` attribute.

Example:

HTML File (`index.html`):

```html
<!DOCTYPE html>
<html lang="en">
<head>
  <meta charset="UTF-8">
  <meta name="viewport" content="width=device-width, initial-scale=1.0">
  <title>External JavaScript Example</title>
```

```
  <script src="script.js" defer></script>
</head>
<body>
  <h1>Hello, External JavaScript!</h1>
  <button id="myButton">Click Me</button>
</body>
</html>
```

JavaScript File (`script.js`):

```javascript
document.addEventListener('DOMContentLoaded', function() {
  const button = document.getElementById('myButton');
  button.addEventListener('click', function() {
    alert('Button was clicked!');
  });
});
```

In this example:

- The `<script>` tag in `index.html` links to the external JavaScript file `script.js`.

- The JavaScript file waits for the DOM to load and then adds an event listener to the button with `id="myButton"`.

12.2 DOM Manipulation

The DOM (Document Object Model) represents the structure of an HTML document as a tree of objects. JavaScript allows you to manipulate these objects to dynamically change the content, structure, and style of a web page.

Key DOM Manipulation Methods:

1. Selecting Elements:

```javascript
// Select an element by ID
const element = document.getElementById('myElement');

// Select elements by class name
const elements = document.getElementsByClassName('myClass');

// Select elements by tag name
const paragraphs = document.getElementsByTagName('p');

// Select elements using a CSS selector
const queryElement = document.querySelector('.myClass');
```

2. Modifying Content:

```javascript
// Change the text content of an element
const heading = document.getElementById('myHeading');
heading.textContent = 'New Heading Text';

// Change the HTML content of an element
const container = document.getElementById('myContainer');
container.innerHTML = '<p>New paragraph content</p>';
```

```
```

3. Changing Styles:

```javascript
// Change the style of an element
const box = document.getElementById('myBox');
box.style.backgroundColor = 'blue';
box.style.color = 'white';
```

4. Creating and Appending Elements:

```javascript
// Create a new element
const newParagraph = document.createElement('p');
newParagraph.textContent = 'This is a new paragraph.';

// Append the new element to an existing element
const content = document.getElementById('content');
content.appendChild(newParagraph);
```

Example:

```html
<!DOCTYPE html>
<html lang="en">
<head>
```

```html
    <meta charset="UTF-8">
    <meta name="viewport" content="width=device-width, initial-scale=1.0">
    <title>DOM Manipulation Example</title>
    <style>
      #content {
        background-color: #f4f4f4;
        padding: 20px;
      }
    </style>
</head>
<body>
  <div id="content">
    <h1 id="myHeading">Original Heading</h1>
    <button onclick="changeContent()">Change Content</button>
  </div>

  <script>
    function changeContent() {
      const heading = document.getElementById('myHeading');
      heading.textContent = 'Updated Heading';

      const newParagraph = document.createElement('p');
      newParagraph.textContent = 'This is a new paragraph added dynamically.';
      document.getElementById('content').appendChild(newParagraph);
    }
  </script>
</body>
</html>
```

In this example:

- The `changeContent()` function updates the text of the heading and appends a new paragraph to the `#content` div when the button is clicked.

12.3 Event Handling in HTML5

Event Handling allows you to execute JavaScript code in response to user actions or other events occurring in the browser.

Common Event Types:

- Mouse Events: `click`, `dblclick`, `mouseover`, `mouseout`

- Keyboard Events: `keydown`, `keyup`, `keypress`

- Form Events: `submit`, `change`, `focus`, `blur`

Adding Event Listeners:

You can attach event listeners to HTML elements using the `addEventListener()` method, which provides more flexibility than using inline event attributes.

Example:

```html
<!DOCTYPE html>
<html lang="en">
<head>
  <meta charset="UTF-8">
  <meta name="viewport" content="width=device-width, initial-scale=1.0">
  <title>Event Handling Example</title>
</head>
```

```
<body>
  <button id="clickButton">Click Me</button>
  <input type="text" id="textInput" placeholder="Type something">

  <script>
    // Adding a click event listener to the button
    document.getElementById('clickButton').addEventListener('click', function() {
      alert('Button was clicked!');
    });

    // Adding a keyup event listener to the input field
    document.getElementById('textInput').addEventListener('keyup', function(event) {
      console.log('Key pressed: ' + event.key);
    });
  </script>
</body>
</html>
```

In this example:

- A click event listener is added to the button with `id="clickButton"`. When the button is clicked, an alert is shown.

- A keyup event listener is added to the input field with `id="textInput"`. Each time a key is released while typing in the input field, the key pressed is logged to the console.

Event Object:

When an event occurs, an event object is created and passed to the event handler. This object contains information about the event, such as the target element and type of event.

Example:

```javascript
document.getElementById('clickButton').addEventListener('click', function(event) {
  console.log('Event type: ' + event.type);
  console.log('Target element: ' + event.target.id);
});
```

In this example:

- The event object provides information about the event, such as its type and the element that triggered it.

Summary:

- Integrating JavaScript with HTML5: JavaScript can be embedded directly in HTML documents or linked as external files to enhance web page functionality.

- DOM Manipulation: JavaScript allows for dynamic changes to the HTML structure, content, and style of a page through the DOM API.

- Event Handling: JavaScript can respond to user interactions and other events by attaching event listeners to elements and handling events with JavaScript code.

Combining JavaScript with HTML5 enables developers to create interactive and dynamic web applications that enhance user experience and engagement.

1. Question: How do you link an external JavaScript file to an HTML document?

- a) `<script src="file.js"></script>`

- b) `<link src="file.js" />`

- c) `<include src="file.js"></include>`

- d) `<import src="file.js"></import>`

Answer: a) `<script src="file.js"></script>`

2. Question: Which of the following is the correct way to write an inline JavaScript function in HTML5?

- a) `<script function="myFunction()">`

- b) `<script type="text/javascript"> function myFunction() { }</script>`

- c) `<js> function myFunction() { }</js>`

- d) `<script language="javascript"> function myFunction() { }</script>`

Answer: b) `<script type="text/javascript"> function myFunction() { }</script>`

3. Question: What attribute should be added to a `<script>` tag to ensure the script is executed after the HTML has been fully parsed?

- a) `defer`

- b) `async`

- c) `delay`

- d) `load`

Answer: a) `defer`

DOM Manipulation

4. Question: Which method is used to select an HTML element by its ID?

  - a) `document.querySelector("#id")`

  - b) `document.getElementByName("id")`

  - c) `document.getElementById("id")`

  - d) `document.getElementByClassName("id")`

  Answer: c) `document.getElementById("id")`

5. Question: What method is used to create a new HTML element in the DOM?

  - a) `document.createElement()`

  - b) `document.newElement()`

  - c) `document.appendElement()`

  - d) `document.buildElement()`

  Answer: a) `document.createElement()`

6. Question: Which of the following methods adds a new child node to an existing element?

  - a) `element.appendChild()`

  - b) `element.addChild()`

  - c) `element.insertChild()`

  - d) `element.newChild()`

  Answer: a) `element.appendChild()`

Event Handling in HTML5

7. Question: How do you add an event listener to an HTML element in JavaScript?

  - a) `element.listenEvent("click", function)`

  - b) `element.addEventListener("click", function)`

- c) `element.on("click", function)`

- d) `element.addEvent("click", function)`

Answer: b) `element.addEventListener("click", function)`

8. Question: Which event is triggered when the DOM is fully loaded and parsed?

  - a) `load`

  - b) `DOMContentLoaded`

  - c) `DOMContentLoad`

  - d) `ready`

  Answer: b) `DOMContentLoaded`

9. Question: What method can be used to stop the event propagation?

  - a) `event.stopPropagation()`

  - b) `event.preventPropagation()`

  - c) `event.haltPropagation()`

  - d) `event.cancelPropagation()`

  Answer: a) `event.stopPropagation()`

10. Question: How do you prevent the default action of an event in JavaScript?

  - a) `event.preventDefault()`

  - b) `event.stopDefault()`

  - c) `event.haltDefault()`

  - d) `event.cancelDefault()`

  Answer: a) `event.preventDefault()`

13. Accessibility in HTML5

   - Importance of Web Accessibility

   - Using ARIA Roles and Properties

   - Best Practices for Accessible Web Design

13. Accessibility in HTML5

Web Accessibility ensures that websites and web applications are usable by people with various disabilities. HTML5 offers several features and best practices to enhance accessibility and make web content more inclusive.

Importance of Web Accessibility

Web accessibility is crucial for several reasons:

Inclusivity: It ensures that people with disabilities can access and interact with web content, which promotes equality and inclusivity.

Legal Compliance: Many countries have legal requirements for web accessibility, such as the Americans with Disabilities Act (ADA) in the United States or the Web Content Accessibility Guidelines (WCAG) internationally.

Improved Usability: Accessible design often improves usability for all users, including those on mobile devices, aging populations, or those with temporary impairments.

Example:

An accessible website might include features like screen reader compatibility, keyboard navigation, and proper contrast ratios. This ensures that users with visual impairments, motor impairments, or cognitive disabilities can effectively use the site.

Using ARIA Roles and Properties

ARIA (Accessible Rich Internet Applications) roles and properties enhance accessibility by providing additional information about web elements, especially for users who rely on assistive technologies like screen readers.

ARIA Roles:

Role Attributes: Define the type of content an element represents.

  - `<div role="navigation">` indicates that the div is used for navigation.

  - `<button role="button">` specifies that the element is a button.

ARIA Properties:

- `aria-label`: Provides a label for an element when text content is not sufficient.
  ```html
  <button aria-label="Close">X</button>
  ```

Here, the `aria-label` attribute provides a textual description for the button.

- `aria-labelledby`: References another element that provides a label.
  ```html
  <div id="label1">Important Information</div>
  <div aria-labelledby="label1">Content related to the important information</div>
  ```

- `aria-live`: Indicates how updates to an element should be announced by assistive technologies.
  ```html
  <div aria-live="polite">Live content updates</div>
  ```

Example:

```
<button role="button" aria-label="Submit Form">Submit</button>
```

In this example, the `aria-label` attribute helps screen readers understand the button's purpose, which might not be obvious from the visual content alone.

Best Practices for Accessible Web Design

1. Use Semantic HTML:

Semantic HTML elements convey meaning about the content and structure of a web page. This helps assistive technologies understand the content better.

Example:

```
<header>
  <h1>Welcome to Our Website</h1>
</header>
<main>
  <section>
    <h2>About Us</h2>
    <p>We are a web development company...</p>
  </section>
  <footer>
    <p>&copy; 2024 Our Company</p>
  </footer>
</main>
```

Using semantic elements like **\<header\>**, **\<main\>**, **\<section\>**, and **\<footer\>** improves the document's structure and accessibility.

Provide Text Alternatives:

Ensure that non-text content, such as images and videos, has text alternatives that convey the same meaning.

Example:

```
<img src="logo.png" alt="Company Logo">
```

The **alt** attribute provides a description of the image, which is read by screen readers.

3. Ensure Keyboard Accessibility:

All interactive elements should be accessible via keyboard. This includes providing proper focus management and ensuring that keyboard navigation is intuitive.

Example:

```
<a href="#content" tabindex="0">Skip to content</a>
```

The **tabindex="0"** attribute ensures that the link is focusable via keyboard navigation, allowing users to quickly skip to the main content.

4. Use Color with Care:

Ensure sufficient contrast between text and background colors to support users with visual impairments. Avoid using color alone to convey important information.

Example:

```
<style>
 .high-contrast {
  color: #000000; /* Black text */
  background-color: #FFFFFF; /* White background */
 }
</style>
<p class="high-contrast">This text has high contrast for readability.</p>
```

Implement Accessible Forms:

Label form elements clearly and ensure that they are correctly associated with their respective controls.

Example:

```
<form>
 <label for="email">Email:</label>
```

```
<input type="email" id="email" name="email" required>
<button type="submit">Submit</button>
</form>
```
```

The **for** attribute of the **<label>** tag links it to the corresponding **<input>** field, enhancing accessibility.

**Provide Clear and Consistent Navigation:**

Ensure that navigation menus are easy to understand and use. Consistent navigation across the site improves usability for all users.

**Example:**

```
<nav>
 <ul>
  <li><a href="#home">Home</a></li>
  <li><a href="#services">Services</a></li>
  <li><a href="#contact">Contact</a></li>
 </ul>
</nav>
```

Summary:

Importance of Web Accessibility: Web accessibility ensures that content is usable by people with disabilities and is often required by law. It also improves overall usability.
```

Using ARIA Roles and Properties: ARIA roles and properties enhance accessibility by providing additional context to assistive technologies.

Best Practices for Accessible Web Design: Use semantic HTML, provide text alternatives, ensure keyboard accessibility, use color with care, implement accessible forms, and maintain clear navigation to create an inclusive web experience.

By adhering to these best practices, developers can create web content that is accessible to a broader audience, ensuring that everyone can engage with and benefit from the web.

14. SEO and HTML5

- ✓ **SEO Basics and HTML5**
- ✓ **Optimizing HTML5 for Search Engines**
- ✓ **Rich Snippets and Microdata**

SEO

Search Engine Optimization (SEO) is the process of improving a website's visibility in search engine results pages (SERPs). HTML5 offers various features and best practices that can enhance SEO efforts and improve the ranking of web pages. This section explores SEO basics in the context of HTML5, techniques for optimizing HTML5 content for search engines, and the use of rich snippets and microdata.

SEO Basics:

SEO involves optimizing various aspects of a website to make it more attractive to search engines. Key SEO factors include:

Keyword Research: Identifying and using relevant keywords that users are likely to search for.

On-Page SEO: Optimizing individual web pages to rank higher and earn more relevant traffic.

Off-Page SEO: Improving a site's authority and relevance through external methods like backlinks.

Technical SEO: Ensuring that a website meets technical requirements such as site speed, mobile-friendliness, and secure connections.

HTML5 and SEO:

HTML5 enhances SEO by offering new elements and attributes that help search engines understand the content and structure of a page. Proper use of these elements can improve a site's visibility and ranking.

Example:

```html
<!DOCTYPE html>
<html lang="en">
<head>
  <meta charset="UTF-8">
  <meta name="description" content="Learn HTML5 and SEO basics with this comprehensive guide.">
  <meta name="keywords" content="HTML5, SEO, search engine optimization">
  <title>HTML5 and SEO Basics</title>
</head>
<body>
  <header>
    <h1>Understanding HTML5 and SEO</h1>
  </header>
  <main>
    <section>
      <h2>What is SEO?</h2>
      <p>SEO stands for Search Engine Optimization...</p>
    </section>
  </main>
  <footer>
    <p>&copy; 2024 SEO Guide</p>
  </footer>
</body>
</html>
```

In this example:

The **<meta>** tags in the **<head>** section provide search engines with a description and keywords relevant to the content of the page.

The **<title>** tag specifies the title of the page, which appears in search engine results and browser tabs.

Optimizing HTML5 for Search Engines

Use Semantic HTML:

Semantic HTML5 elements like `<header>`, `<nav>`, `<main>`, `<section>`, and `<footer>` help search engines understand the structure and main content of a page.

Example:

```
<header>
 <h1>Top 10 Tips for SEO</h1>
 <nav>
  <ul>
   <li><a href="#tips">SEO Tips</a></li>
   <li><a href="#tools">SEO Tools</a></li>
  </ul>
 </nav>
</header>
<main>
 <section id="tips">
  <h2>1. Keyword Research</h2>
  <p>Effective keyword research is crucial for SEO...</p>
 </section>
 <section id="tools">
  <h2>2. SEO Tools</h2>
```

```
    <p>Various tools can help with SEO...</p>
  </section>
</main>
```

Optimize Page Titles and Meta Descriptions:

Page Titles: Include relevant keywords and keep titles concise (50-60 characters).

Meta Descriptions: Provide a summary of the page content (150-160 characters) and include keywords.

Example:

```
<head>
  <title>Top 10 SEO Tips for 2024 | SEO Guide</title>
  <meta name="description" content="Discover the top 10 SEO tips for 2024 to boost your website's ranking and visibility.">
</head>
```

Use Header Tags Appropriately:

Header tags (**<h1>**, **<h2>**, **<h3>**, etc.) structure the content hierarchically, making it easier for search engines to understand the main topics and subtopics.

Example:

```
<h1>Ultimate Guide to SEO</h1>
<h2>1. Understanding SEO</h2>
<h3>1.1 Keyword Research</h3>
<h2>2. SEO Best Practices</h2>
```

Optimize Images with Alt Text:

Use the `alt` attribute to describe images. This helps search engines understand the content of images and improves accessibility.

Example:

```
<img src="seo-tips.jpg" alt="A guide to SEO tips and best practices">
```

Implement Responsive Design:

Ensure your website is mobile-friendly by using responsive design techniques. This improves user experience and can positively impact search rankings.

Example:

```
<meta name="viewport" content="width=device-width, initial-scale=1.0">
```

Improve Site Speed:

Optimize loading times by compressing images, minimizing CSS and JavaScript, and leveraging browser caching.

Example:

```
<link rel="stylesheet" href="styles.css">
<script src="script.js" defer></script>
```

Rich Snippets and Microdata

Rich Snippets:

Rich snippets are enhanced search results that provide additional information to users, such as reviews, ratings, and prices. They are generated using structured data markup.

Microdata:

Microdata is a way to add structured data to HTML5 elements, making it easier for search engines to parse and understand the content. This data is often used to generate rich snippets in search results.

Example of Microdata:

```html
<!DOCTYPE html>
<html lang="en">
<head>
  <meta charset="UTF-8">
  <meta name="viewport" content="width=device-width, initial-scale=1.0">
  <title>Product Page</title>
</head>
<body>
  <div itemscope itemtype="http://schema.org/Product">
    <h1 itemprop="name">Awesome Widget</h1>
    <img itemprop="image" src="widget.jpg" alt="Awesome Widget">
    <p itemprop="description">The Awesome Widget is the best widget you'll ever need.</p>
    <span itemprop="offers" itemscope itemtype="http://schema.org/Offer">
      <span itemprop="priceCurrency" content="USD">$</span>
      <span itemprop="price" content="29.99">29.99</span>
    </span>
  </div>
</body>
</html>
```

In this example:

- **itemscope** and **itemtype** define the type of data being described (a product).

- **itemprop** attributes specify the properties of the product, such as its name, image, description, and price.

Benefits of Rich Snippets:

Enhanced Visibility: Rich snippets can make search results more attractive and informative, potentially increasing click-through rates.

Improved Relevance: By providing additional context, rich snippets help users find relevant information more easily.

Summary:

SEO Basics and HTML5: HTML5 offers features that enhance SEO, such as semantic elements, meta tags, and proper use of headers.

Optimizing HTML5 for Search Engines: Utilize semantic HTML, optimize page titles and meta descriptions, use header tags appropriately, optimize images, implement responsive design, and improve site speed.

Rich Snippets and Microdata: Rich snippets provide additional information in search results through structured data, which can be implemented using microdata to enhance visibility and relevance.

By following these best practices and utilizing HTML5 features, developers can improve their site's SEO, making it more visible and attractive to both search engines and users.

15. Performance Optimization

- ✓ **Minimizing HTML5 File Sizes**
- ✓ **Best Practices for Fast Loading Times**
- ✓ **Tools and Techniques for Performance Testing**

Performance Optimization

Performance optimization is critical for delivering a fast, efficient, and smooth user experience. In the context of HTML5, optimizing web performance involves minimizing file sizes, implementing best practices for fast loading times, and using tools and techniques for performance testing. Here's a detailed guide on each of these topics.

Minimizing HTML5 File Sizes

Reducing file sizes is essential for faster page load times and improved user experience. This involves optimizing various components of an HTML5 document:

Minify HTML Code:

Minification involves removing unnecessary characters from HTML code without changing its functionality. This includes removing whitespace, comments, and redundant attributes.

Example:

Before Minification:

```
<!DOCTYPE html>
<html lang="en">
<head>
 <meta charset="UTF-8">
 <meta name="viewport" content="width=device-width, initial-scale=1.0">
 <title>Performance Optimization</title>
</head>
<body>
 <header>
```

```
    <h1>Welcome to Performance Optimization</h1>
  </header>
  <main>
    <section>
      <p>This section contains information about performance optimization.</p>
    </section>
  </main>
  <footer>
    <p>&copy; 2024 Performance Optimization</p>
  </footer>
</body>
</html>
```

After Minification:

```
<!DOCTYPE html><html lang="en"><head><meta charset="UTF-8"><meta name="viewport" content="width=device-width, initial-scale=1.0"><title>Performance Optimization</title></head><body><header><h1>Welcome to Performance Optimization</h1></header><main><section><p>This section contains information about performance optimization.</p></section></main><footer><p>&copy; 2024 Performance Optimization</p></footer></body></html>
```

Optimize Images:

Use image formats like WebP for better compression and faster loading times. Compress images to reduce their size while maintaining quality.

Example:

Before Compression:

```
<img src="large-image.jpg" alt="Large Image">
```

After Compression:

```
<img src="large-image.webp" alt="Optimized Image">
```

Use Efficient Fonts:

Limit the number of web fonts used and ensure that font files are optimized. Use the `font-display` property to control font loading.

Example:

```
<link rel="stylesheet"
href="https://fonts.googleapis.com/css2?family=Roboto:wght@400;700&display=swap">
```

Best Practices for Fast Loading Times

Implement Browser Caching:

Leverage browser caching to store static resources like images, CSS, and JavaScript files on the user's device. This reduces the need for repeated downloads on subsequent visits.

Example:

```
<!-- Cache-Control header in server response -->
Cache-Control: max-age=31536000
```

Minimize HTTP Requests:

Reduce the number of HTTP requests by combining CSS and JavaScript files, and using image sprites.

Example:

Combining CSS Files:

Before:

```
<link rel="stylesheet" href="styles1.css">
<link rel="stylesheet" href="styles2.css">
```

After:

```
<link rel="stylesheet" href="combined-styles.css">
```

Use Asynchronous Loading for JavaScript:

Load JavaScript files asynchronously or defer their loading to prevent them from blocking the rendering of the page.

Example:

```
<script src="script.js" async></script>
```

Optimize CSS Delivery:

Inline critical CSS to render above-the-fold content quickly and load non-critical CSS asynchronously.

Example:

Inline Critical CSS:

```
<style>
 /* Critical CSS */
 body { font-family: Arial, sans-serif; }
</style>
```

Load Non-Critical CSS Asynchronously:

```
<link rel="stylesheet" href="non-critical.css" media="print" onload="this.media='all'">
```

Enable Compression:

Use Gzip or Brotli compression to reduce the size of files sent from the server to the client.

Example:

Gzip Compression:

```
<!-- Server Configuration -->
AddOutputFilterByType DEFLATE text/html
```

Tools and Techniques for Performance Testing

Google PageSpeed Insights:

Google PageSpeed Insights analyzes the content of a web page and provides suggestions for improving performance. It offers both mobile and desktop performance scores and recommendations.

Example:

Visit [PageSpeed Insights](https://developers.google.com/speed/pagespeed/insights/) and enter your URL to get a performance report.

Lighthouse:

Lighthouse is an open-source, automated tool for improving the quality of web pages. It provides audits for performance, accessibility, SEO, and more.

Example:

To use Lighthouse in Chrome:

Open Chrome DevTools (F12 or right-click on the page and select "Inspect").

Go to the "Lighthouse" tab.

Click "Generate report" to get performance insights.

WebPageTest:

WebPageTest allows you to test your website's performance from different locations and browsers. It provides detailed performance metrics and suggestions for improvement.

Example:

Visit [WebPageTest](https://www.webpagetest.org/) and enter your URL to perform a performance test.

GTmetrix:

GTmetrix combines Google Lighthouse and WebPageTest to provide a comprehensive performance report. It offers insights into page load times and recommendations for optimization.

Example:

Visit [GTmetrix](https://gtmetrix.com/) and enter your URL to analyze your website's performance.

Performance Timing API:

The Performance Timing API allows you to measure various performance metrics programmatically, such as page load times and navigation events.

Example:

```
window.addEventListener('load', () => {
  const timing = window.performance.timing;
  console.log('Page Load Time:', timing.loadEventEnd - timing.navigationStart);
});
```

Summary:

Minimizing HTML5 File Sizes: Minify HTML code, optimize images, and use efficient fonts to reduce file sizes and improve loading times.

Best Practices for Fast Loading Times: Implement browser caching, minimize HTTP requests, use asynchronous JavaScript loading, optimize CSS delivery, and enable compression.

Tools and Techniques for Performance Testing: Use tools like Google PageSpeed Insights, Lighthouse, WebPageTest, GTmetrix, and the Performance Timing API to test and improve website performance.

By applying these performance optimization techniques, you can create a faster, more efficient website that provides a better user experience and performs well in search engine rankings.

16. Projects and Case Studies

Building a Responsive Website

- Planning and Wireframing

- Implementing a Responsive Layout

- Testing and Debugging

Building a Responsive Website

Creating a responsive website ensures that it provides an optimal viewing experience across a variety of devices, from desktops to mobile phones. This involves planning and wireframing, implementing a responsive layout, and thorough testing and debugging. Below is a detailed guide on each of these steps.

Planning and Wireframing

Understanding Project Requirements:

Before starting the design, gather and understand the project requirements. This includes defining the target audience, identifying key functionalities, and establishing design goals.

Example:

Client Needs: A website for a local bakery that must be accessible on both desktop and mobile devices.

Key Functionalities: Online menu, contact form, and location map.

Creating a Wireframe:

Wireframing involves sketching the basic layout and structure of the website. This helps visualize the placement of elements such as headers, navigation menus, content areas, and footers.

Tools for Wireframing:

Paper and Pencil: Simple and effective for initial sketches.

Digital Tools: Tools like Adobe XD, Figma, and Sketch offer advanced wireframing capabilities.

Example Wireframe:

Header

Navigation	Search	Contact Info

Main Content Area

Hero Image

Welcome Text

Call To Action

Footer

Address	Social Media Links

Designing Mobile and Desktop Views:

Create separate wireframes for mobile and desktop views to ensure that all elements are appropriately adapted for different screen sizes.

Example:

Desktop View: Wide layout with multiple columns.

Mobile View: Single-column layout with stacked elements.

Implementing a Responsive Layout

Setting Up the HTML Structure:

Create the basic HTML structure according to the wireframe. Use semantic HTML5 elements to ensure clear and meaningful content organization.

Example:

```
<!DOCTYPE html>
<html lang="en">
<head>
 <meta charset="UTF-8">
 <meta name="viewport" content="width=device-width, initial-scale=1.0">
 <title>Responsive Bakery Website</title>
 <link rel="stylesheet" href="styles.css">
</head>
<body>
 <header>
  <h1>Local Bakery</h1>
  <nav>
```

```html
    <ul>
        <li><a href="#home">Home</a></li>
        <li><a href="#menu">Menu</a></li>
        <li><a href="#contact">Contact</a></li>
    </ul>
  </nav>
</header>
<main>
  <section id="home">
    <img src="hero.jpg" alt="Delicious Bakery Items">
    <h2>Welcome to Our Bakery!</h2>
    <button>Order Now</button>
  </section>
  <section id="menu">
    <h2>Our Menu</h2>
    <!-- Menu items -->
  </section>
  <section id="contact">
    <h2>Contact Us</h2>
    <!-- Contact form -->
  </section>
</main>
<footer>
  <p>&copy; 2024 Local Bakery</p>
</footer>
</body>
</html>
```

Applying CSS for Responsiveness:

Use CSS to create a responsive design. The key techniques include:

Fluid Grids: Use percentage-based widths for layout elements.

Example:

```css
.container {
  width: 80%;
  margin: 0 auto;
}
```

Media Queries: Apply different styles for different screen sizes.

Example:

```css
/* Default styles for desktop */
body {
  font-size: 16px;
}

/* Styles for mobile devices */
@media (max-width: 600px) {
  body {
    font-size: 14px;
```

```
  }
  header {
    text-align: center;

  }

}
```

Flexible Images: Ensure images scale with their containers.

Example:

```
img {
  max-width: 100%;
  height: auto;

}
```

Implementing Responsive Navigation:

Use techniques such as collapsible menus or hamburger icons to make navigation mobile-friendly.

Example:

```
<!-- Navigation Menu -->
<nav>
  <button class="menu-toggle" aria-label="Open Menu">☰</button>
  <ul class="menu">
```

```
  <li><a href="#home">Home</a></li>

  <li><a href="#menu">Menu</a></li>

  <li><a href="#contact">Contact</a></li>

 </ul>

</nav>
```

CSS for Responsive Menu:

```
.menu {
  display: none;
}


.menu-toggle {
  display: block;
}


@media (min-width: 600px) {
  .menu {
    display: flex;
  }
  .menu-toggle {
    display: none;
  }
}
```

Testing and Debugging

Cross-Browser Testing:

Ensure the website functions correctly across different browsers (Chrome, Firefox, Safari, Edge). Tools like BrowserStack can help with cross-browser testing.

Example:

Test interactive elements, layout, and media on different browsers to identify inconsistencies.

Responsive Testing:

Check how the website performs on various screen sizes and devices. Use browser developer tools to simulate different devices and viewports.

Example:

In Chrome Developer Tools, use the "Toggle Device Toolbar" to test mobile and tablet views.

Performance Testing:

Evaluate the website's loading speed and responsiveness using tools like Google PageSpeed Insights or GTmetrix. Address any performance issues identified.

Example:

Optimize images and minify CSS/JavaScript files if the performance tests indicate slow load times.

Accessibility Testing:

Ensure the website is accessible to users with disabilities. Use tools like WAVE or Axe to identify and fix accessibility issues.

Example:

Check color contrast, keyboard navigation, and screen reader compatibility.

Debugging:

Address any bugs or issues identified during testing. Use browser developer tools to inspect and debug HTML, CSS, and JavaScript.

Example:

Use the Console and Sources tabs in Chrome Developer Tools to debug JavaScript errors and review code execution.

Summary:

Planning and Wireframing: Define project requirements, create wireframes for both desktop and mobile views, and plan the layout and functionality.

Implementing a Responsive Layout: Set up HTML structure, apply responsive CSS techniques, and implement mobile-friendly navigation.

Testing and Debugging: Perform cross-browser and responsive testing, evaluate performance, ensure accessibility, and debug issues using various tools.

By following these steps, you can build a responsive website that provides an optimal user experience across all devices and screen sizes.

17. HTML5 Game Development

- ✓ **Introduction to Game Development with HTML5**
- ✓ **Using Canvas for Game Graphics**
- ✓ **Interactive Game Logic with JavaScript**

HTML5 Game Development

HTML5 has significantly transformed game development, providing powerful tools to create engaging and interactive web-based games. This section covers the essentials of HTML5 game development, including an introduction to game development with HTML5, using Canvas for game graphics, and implementing interactive game logic with JavaScript.

Introduction to Game Development with HTML5

What is HTML5 Game Development?

HTML5 game development involves creating games that run directly in web browsers using HTML5 technologies. Unlike traditional game development, which often relies on plugins or standalone applications, HTML5 games leverage the built-in capabilities of modern browsers, making them accessible across various devices and platforms.

Key Technologies:

HTML5: Provides the structure and elements needed for the game.

CSS3: Used for styling game elements.

JavaScript: Handles game logic, interactivity, and rendering.

Benefits of HTML5 Game Development:

Cross-Platform Compatibility: HTML5 games work on desktops, tablets, and smartphones.

No Plugins Required: Games run directly in the browser without additional plugins.

Easy Distribution: Games can be easily shared and played online.

Example:

Imagine creating a simple browser-based game like a "Flappy Bird" clone using HTML5. The game would use HTML5 for the game canvas, CSS3 for styling, and JavaScript for game mechanics.

Using Canvas for Game Graphics

Introduction to <canvas>:

The <canvas> element in HTML5 provides a drawable region in a web page, which is ideal for rendering game graphics. It allows developers to draw shapes, text, images, and other visual elements using JavaScript.

Basic Canvas Setup:

```html
<!DOCTYPE html>
<html lang="en">
<head>
 <meta charset="UTF-8">
 <meta name="viewport" content="width=device-width, initial-scale=1.0">
 <title>HTML5 Game Canvas</title>
 <style>
  canvas {
   border: 1px solid #000;
  }
 </style>
</head>
<body>
 <canvas id="gameCanvas" width="800" height="600"></canvas>
```

```
 <script src="game.js"></script>
</body>
</html>
```

Drawing on the Canvas:

Use JavaScript to access the canvas and its drawing context. The 2D rendering context allows you to draw shapes and images.

Example Code:

```
const canvas = document.getElementById('gameCanvas');
const ctx = canvas.getContext('2d');


// Draw a rectangle
ctx.fillStyle = 'blue';
ctx.fillRect(50, 50, 150, 100);
// Draw a circle
ctx.beginPath();
ctx.arc(200, 200, 50, 0, Math.PI * 2);
ctx.fillStyle = 'red';
ctx.fill();
```

Animation with Canvas:

Animating game graphics involves repeatedly redrawing the canvas at a set interval.

Example Code:

```javascript
let x = 0;

function animate() {

  ctx.clearRect(0, 0, canvas.width, canvas.height); // Clear canvas

  ctx.fillStyle = 'green';

  ctx.fillRect(x, 100, 50, 50); // Draw rectangle


  x += 5; // Move rectangle

  if (x > canvas.width) x = 0; // Reset position


  requestAnimationFrame(animate); // Schedule next frame

}


animate(); // Start animation
```

Interactive Game Logic with JavaScript

Handling User Input:

JavaScript can capture user input from the keyboard or mouse, enabling player interaction within the game.

Example Code:

```javascript
document.addEventListener('keydown', (event) => {

  if (event.key === 'ArrowUp') {

    // Move player up
```

```
} else if (event.key === 'ArrowDown') {

  // Move player down

  }

});
```

Game Loop:

A game loop continuously updates the game state and renders frames. It is crucial for maintaining a smooth gaming experience.

Example Code:

```
function gameLoop() {

  updateGame(); // Update game logic

  renderGame(); // Render game graphics

  requestAnimationFrame(gameLoop); // Continue game loop

}

function updateGame() {

  // Update game state (e.g., player position)

}

function renderGame() {

  // Clear canvas and redraw game elements

}

gameLoop(); // Start game loop
```

Collision Detection:

Detecting collisions between game objects is essential for gameplay mechanics.

Example Code:

```
function checkCollision(obj1, obj2) {
  return obj1.x < obj2.x + obj2.width &&
      obj1.x + obj1.width > obj2.x &&
      obj1.y < obj2.y + obj2.height &&
      obj1.y + obj1.height > obj2.y;
}
```

Game State Management:

Manage different states of the game, such as starting, playing, and ending states.

Example Code:

```
let gameState = 'start';
```

```
function updateGame() {
  if (gameState === 'start') {
    // Initialize game
  } else if (gameState === 'playing') {
    // Update game elements
  } else if (gameState === 'end') {
    // Display game over screen
  }
}
```

Scoring and Levels:

Implement scoring systems and game levels to enhance gameplay.

Example Code:

```
let score = 0;

function updateScore(points) {
  score += points;
  document.getElementById('score').textContent = `Score: ${score}`;
}

function levelUp() {
  // Increase difficulty and/or progress to next level
}
```

Summary:

Introduction to Game Development with HTML5: HTML5 game development uses HTML, CSS, and JavaScript to create browser-based games. It offers cross-platform compatibility and eliminates the need for plugins.

Using Canvas for Game Graphics: The `<canvas>` element and its 2D rendering context allow developers to draw and animate game graphics. Basic drawing, animation, and rendering techniques are essential.

Interactive Game Logic with JavaScript: JavaScript enables handling user input, managing game loops, detecting collisions, and maintaining game states. Interactive and dynamic elements are crucial for engaging gameplay.

By understanding and applying these concepts, you can develop interactive and visually appealing games that run smoothly across different devices and browsers.

18. Real-World Case Studies

- ✓ **Examples of Successful HTML5 Websites**
- ✓ **Analyzing and Learning from Case Studies**

Real-World Case Studies

Real-world case studies offer valuable insights into how HTML5 technologies are effectively utilized to build successful and innovative websites. This section explores examples of successful HTML5 websites and provides an analysis of these case studies to extract key lessons and best practices.

Examples of Successful HTML5 Websites

1. Awwwards (https://www.awwwards.com)

Awwwards is a platform that showcases and awards outstanding websites from around the world. It highlights the best in design, creativity, and innovation, many of which use advanced HTML5 features.

Features and Innovations:

Responsive Design: Websites featured on Awwwards are often optimized for various devices and screen sizes.

Interactive Elements: Advanced use of HTML5 APIs, such as Canvas for animations and WebGL for 3D graphics.

High-Quality Graphics: Implementation of SVG and CSS3 for crisp and scalable graphics.

Example Analysis:

Interactive Animations: Websites use Canvas and CSS animations to create engaging visual effects.

Responsive Layouts: Fluid grids and media queries ensure compatibility across devices.

CodePen (https://codepen.io)

CodePen is a social development environment for front-end designers and developers. It allows users to showcase their HTML5, CSS3, and JavaScript code snippets.

Features and Innovations:

Live Previews: Real-time preview of code changes, showcasing dynamic HTML5 features.

Community Contributions: Users share and learn from interactive HTML5 examples and experiments.

Example Analysis:

Code Examples: Provides real-world examples of HTML5 capabilities, such as new input types and APIs.

Community Engagement: Encourages collaboration and learning through shared projects and feedback.

The New York Times (https://www.nytimes.com)

The New York Times website utilizes HTML5 to enhance user experience with multimedia content and interactive features.

Features and Innovations:

Interactive Stories: Use of HTML5 video and audio for immersive storytelling.

Responsive Design: Adaptation of content for various devices using flexible layouts and media queries.

Example Analysis:

Rich Media Integration: Seamless integration of videos, infographics, and interactive graphics.

Content Adaptation: Ensures readability and usability across different screen sizes and orientations.

Analyzing and Learning from Case Studies

Identifying Best Practices

Responsive Design:

Lesson: Successful websites prioritize responsive design to ensure usability across all devices.

Application: Implement fluid grids, flexible images, and media queries to adapt layouts and content.

Performance Optimization:

Lesson: Speed and performance are critical for user engagement and satisfaction.

Application: Minimize file sizes, leverage caching, and optimize images and scripts for faster loading times.

Interactive Features:

Lesson: Engaging user interactions can significantly enhance the user experience.

Application: Utilize HTML5 APIs, such as Canvas for animations and Geolocation for personalized content.

Analyzing Design and Functionality

Design Aesthetics:

Lesson: Visual appeal and user-friendly design are crucial for retaining visitors.

Application: Apply modern design principles, such as minimalism, high-quality visuals, and intuitive navigation.

Functionality and Usability:

Lesson: Functional and accessible websites improve user experience and engagement.

Application: Ensure that all features are fully functional, accessible, and provide clear instructions and feedback.

Technical Considerations

HTML5 APIs:

Lesson: Leveraging HTML5 APIs enhances functionality and interactivity.

Application: Implement APIs such as Web Storage for persistent data and WebRTC for real-time communication.

Cross-Browser Compatibility:

Lesson: Consistent performance across different browsers and devices is essential.

Application: Test and optimize for various browsers to ensure a uniform experience.

Learning from Failures

Case Study Analysis:

Lesson: Analyzing websites that failed to meet user expectations can reveal common pitfalls.

Application: Avoid issues like slow loading times, poor mobile optimization, and complex navigation.

Example of Failure:

Website: A website with heavy use of images and videos that did not optimize file sizes, resulting in slow loading times and high bounce rates.

Applying Insights

Case Study Implementation:

Lesson: Apply insights from successful case studies to your projects to enhance design and functionality.

Application: Use best practices and technologies showcased in successful websites to achieve similar success.

Summary:

Examples of Successful HTML5 Websites: Explore websites like Awwwards, CodePen, and The New York Times to see how HTML5 is used effectively in real-world applications.

Analyzing and Learning from Case Studies: Identify best practices, analyze design and functionality, consider technical aspects, and learn from failures to apply insights to your own projects.

By examining these case studies and applying the lessons learned, you can develop effective, engaging, and high-performing HTML5 websites that meet user expectations and stand out in the digital landscape.

19. Future of HTML5

- ✓ **Upcoming Features and Specifications**
- ✓ **HTML5 in Emerging Technologies**

As HTML5 continues to evolve, it remains at the forefront of web development, shaping how websites and web applications are built and experienced. This section explores the future of HTML5, including upcoming features and specifications, and its role in emerging technologies.

Upcoming Features and Specifications

HTML5 Specifications Evolution

The HTML5 specification has undergone numerous updates since its initial release. The ongoing development focuses on refining and expanding the capabilities of HTML5 to meet the growing demands of modern web applications.

Recent and Upcoming Enhancements:

New Elements and Attributes: The HTML Living Standard continually introduces new elements and attributes to improve functionality and usability.

Enhanced APIs: Continuous improvement of existing APIs and introduction of new ones, such as the WebXR API for virtual and augmented reality.

Examples:

Custom Elements: Allow developers to define their own HTML tags and behaviors, enhancing code reusability and modularity.

Shadow DOM: Provides encapsulation for web components, enabling better component isolation and style scoping.

HTML Living Standard

The HTML Living Standard, maintained by the Web Hypertext Application Technology Working Group (WHATWG), represents an ongoing effort to continuously improve HTML. It focuses on implementing practical features that address the needs of modern web development.

Upcoming Features:

Improved Form Controls: Enhancements to input types and attributes to provide better user interaction and validation.

Enhanced Media Capabilities: Support for new media formats and improved handling of multimedia content.

Example:

Native Web Components: Increased support for custom elements, templates, and shadow DOM, allowing for more flexible and reusable UI components.

HTML5 in Emerging Technologies

Integration with Emerging Technologies

HTML5 plays a crucial role in the integration and development of emerging technologies. Its flexibility and robust feature set make it an ideal foundation for new innovations in web development.

Key Areas of Integration:

WebAssembly (Wasm): WebAssembly allows high-performance code to run in the browser. HTML5 serves as the basis for integrating Wasm with traditional web technologies, enabling more complex applications such as games and simulations.

Example:

```
<script>
 // Load WebAssembly module
 fetch('module.wasm')
  .then(response => response.arrayBuffer())
  .then(buffer => WebAssembly.instantiate(buffer))
  .then(module => {
   // Use WebAssembly module
  });
</script>
```

Progressive Web Apps (PWAs): HTML5 provides the essential components for building PWAs, which offer app-like experiences with offline capabilities, push notifications, and home screen access.

Example:

```
// Register service worker for offline capabilities
if ('serviceWorker' in navigator) {
 navigator.serviceWorker.register('/service-worker.js')
  .then(reg => console.log('Service Worker Registered'))
  .catch(err => console.error('Service Worker Registration Failed', err));
}
```

WebRTC: HTML5 supports real-time communication through WebRTC, enabling peer-to-peer video, voice, and data sharing directly within the browser.

Example:

```
const peerConnection = new RTCPeerConnection();
peerConnection.ontrack = event => {
  const remoteStream = event.streams[0];
  document.getElementById('remoteVideo').srcObject = remoteStream;
};
```

Virtual and Augmented Reality: HTML5 APIs, such as WebXR, support immersive experiences by integrating virtual and augmented reality content into web applications.

Example:

```
navigator.xr.requestSession('immersive-vr').then(session => {
  // Initialize VR session
});
```

Enhanced User Experience

HTML5's ongoing advancements contribute to improving user experience by offering more interactive and dynamic web applications.

Examples:

Enhanced Animations and Graphics: Continued development of Canvas and SVG capabilities for richer graphics and animations.

Improved Form Interactions: New input types and validation attributes enhance form usability and user feedback.

Accessibility and Inclusivity

Future HTML5 enhancements will continue to focus on improving accessibility and inclusivity, ensuring that web applications are usable by everyone, including individuals with disabilities.

Example:

ARIA (Accessible Rich Internet Applications): Ongoing improvements to ARIA roles and properties to enhance web accessibility.

Summary:

Upcoming Features and Specifications: The HTML Living Standard and other ongoing updates introduce new elements, APIs, and enhancements to HTML5, improving functionality and usability.

HTML5 in Emerging Technologies: HTML5 integrates seamlessly with emerging technologies such as WebAssembly, PWAs, WebRTC, and WebXR, enabling advanced web applications and immersive experiences.

Enhanced User Experience: Future HTML5 developments will focus on richer graphics, improved form interactions, and better accessibility, contributing to a more dynamic and inclusive web.

HTML5 continues to evolve, shaping the future of web development and expanding its capabilities to meet the needs of modern technology and user expectations. As new features and technologies emerge, HTML5 will remain a fundamental building block for creating innovative and engaging web experiences.

20.Resources and Further Learning

- ✓ **Recommended Books and Online Courses**
- ✓ **Community and Support**

Resources and Further Learning

As you progress in your journey with HTML5, leveraging various resources and communities can enhance your learning and keep you updated with the latest developments. This section provides recommendations for books, online courses, and community support to help you deepen your understanding of HTML5 and stay engaged with the web development community.

Recommended Books and Online Courses

1. Books

a. "HTML and CSS: Design and Build Websites" by Jon Duckett

- Overview: This book offers a visual approach to learning HTML and CSS, making it accessible for beginners and intermediate developers. It covers HTML5 basics, including elements, attributes, and structure, as well as CSS styling and layout techniques.

- Example: The book includes practical examples and exercises to help readers apply concepts in real-world scenarios.

b. "HTML5: The Missing Manual" by Matthew MacDonald

- Overview: This comprehensive guide explores HTML5's new features and capabilities, including multimedia, graphics, and forms. It provides detailed explanations and practical examples to help readers master HTML5.

- Example: Includes in-depth sections on advanced HTML5 features like the Canvas API and Web Storage.

c. "HTML5: Up and Running" by Mark Pilgrim

- Overview: This book provides a hands-on approach to learning HTML5, with a focus on practical applications and real-world examples. It covers essential HTML5 features and APIs, as well as best practices for implementation.

- Example: Offers step-by-step tutorials and code snippets to demonstrate HTML5 concepts.

2. Online Courses

a. "HTML5 and CSS3 Fundamentals" by Udacity

- Overview: This course offers a thorough introduction to HTML5 and CSS3, covering fundamental concepts and techniques. It includes video lectures, interactive quizzes, and practical projects.

- Example: Features projects such as building a responsive webpage and creating multimedia elements with HTML5.

b. "HTML5 Essential Training" by LinkedIn Learning

- Overview: This course provides a comprehensive overview of HTML5, including its new elements, attributes, and APIs. It includes practical exercises and real-world examples to reinforce learning.

- Example: Covers topics such as Canvas drawing, form validation, and integrating multimedia content.

c. "The Complete HTML5 & CSS3 Course Build Professional Websites" by Udemy

- Overview: This course offers an in-depth exploration of HTML5 and CSS3, with a focus on building professional websites. It includes video lectures, hands-on projects, and quizzes.

- Example: Includes practical projects like creating a portfolio website and implementing responsive design techniques.

Community and Support

1. Online Communities

a. Stack Overflow (https://stackoverflow.com)

- Overview: A popular Q&A platform where developers can ask questions, share knowledge, and get solutions to coding problems. It has a large community of HTML5 experts and enthusiasts.

- Example: Users can search for HTML5-related questions and contribute by answering queries or providing solutions.

b. MDN Web Docs Community (https://developer.mozilla.org)

- Overview: Mozilla Developer Network (MDN) provides extensive documentation and resources for web technologies, including HTML5. The community contributes to and maintains the content, offering support and guidance.

- Example: Includes tutorials, reference materials, and examples for HTML5 elements, attributes, and APIs.

c. Reddit Web Development Subreddits (https://www.reddit.com/r/webdev/)

- Overview: Subreddits such as r/webdev and r/frontend provide a space for web developers to discuss HTML5, share resources, and seek advice from peers.

- Example: Users can engage in discussions about the latest HTML5 trends, ask for feedback on projects, and participate in coding challenges.

2. Professional Networks and Meetups

a. Meetup.com (https://www.meetup.com)

- Overview: A platform for organizing and finding local meetups related to web development, including HTML5. It provides opportunities to connect with other developers, attend workshops, and participate in discussions.

- Example: Look for local web development meetups or conferences where HTML5 topics are covered.

b. LinkedIn Groups (https://www.linkedin.com/groups/)

- Overview: LinkedIn groups related to web development and HTML5 offer networking opportunities and professional development. Members can share knowledge, ask questions, and stay updated on industry trends.

- Example: Join groups focused on HTML5 and web development to engage with professionals and stay informed about best practices.

3. Official Documentation and Resources

a. W3C HTML5 Specification (https://www.w3.org/TR/html5/)

- Overview: The World Wide Web Consortium (W3C) provides the official HTML5 specification, including detailed documentation on HTML5 features, elements, and attributes.

- Example: Refer to the specification for in-depth technical details and standards.

b. WHATWG HTML Living Standard (https://html.spec.whatwg.org/multipage/)

- Overview: The Web Hypertext Application Technology Working Group (WHATWG) maintains the HTML Living Standard, offering an up-to-date resource on HTML5 features and updates.

- Example: Use the Living Standard for the latest information and ongoing changes in HTML5.

Summary:

- Recommended Books: "HTML and CSS: Design and Build Websites" by Jon Duckett, "HTML5: The Missing Manual" by Matthew MacDonald, and "HTML5: Up and Running" by Mark Pilgrim provide comprehensive resources for learning HTML5.

- Online Courses: Courses from Udacity, LinkedIn Learning, and Udemy offer structured learning experiences with practical examples and projects.

- Community and Support: Engage with online communities like Stack Overflow, MDN Web Docs, and Reddit for support and knowledge sharing. Participate in professional networks and refer to official documentation for up-to-date information.

By utilizing these resources and engaging with the community, you can continue to advance your knowledge of HTML5, stay current with industry trends, and build a strong foundation for your web development career.

Appendices

- ❖ **HTML5 Cheat Sheet**
- ❖ **Common Tags and Attributes**
- ❖ **Frequently Used Snippets**

An HTML5 cheat sheet is a handy reference for web developers to quickly access common tags, attributes, and frequently used code snippets. It serves as a quick guide to help streamline the development process and ensure that essential HTML5 features are used correctly. Below, we cover the most commonly used HTML5 tags and attributes, as well as frequently used code snippets.

Common Tags and Attributes

1. HTML5 Document Structure Tags

<!DOCTYPE html>: Declares the document type and version of HTML.

```
<!DOCTYPE html>
```

<html>: The root element of an HTML document.

```
<html lang="en">
```

<head>: Contains metadata and links to external resources.

```
<head>
  <meta charset="UTF-8">
  <title>Document Title</title>
  <link rel="stylesheet" href="styles.css">
</head>
```

<body>: Contains the content of the HTML document.

```
<body>
  <h1>Welcome to My Website</h1>
  <p>This is a paragraph of text.</p>
</body>
```

2. Text Formatting Tags

<h1> to <h6>: Header tags for defining headings, with <h1> being the highest level and <h6> the lowest.

```
<h1>Main Heading</h1>
<h2>Subheading</h2>
```

<p>: Defines a paragraph of text.

```
<p>This is a paragraph.</p>
```

<strong>: Emphasizes text with strong importance (bold by default).

```
<strong>Important text</strong>
```

<em>: Emphasizes text (italic by default).

```
<em>Emphasized text</em>
```

3. Links and Lists

<a>: Defines a hyperlink.

```
<a href="https://example.com">Visit Example</a>
```

<ul>: Creates an unordered (bulleted) list.

```
<ul>
  <li>Item 1</li>
  <li>Item 2</li>
</ul>
```

<ol>: Creates an ordered (numbered) list.

```
<ol>
  <li>First item</li>
  <li>Second item</li>
</ol>
```

<dl>: Defines a description list.

```
<dl>
  <dt>Term</dt>
  <dd>Definition</dd>
</dl>
```

4. Images and Media

<img>: Embeds an image.

```
<img src="image.jpg" alt="Description of image">
```

<audio>: Embeds audio content.

```
<audio controls>
  <source src="audio.mp3" type="audio/mpeg">
  Your browser does not support the audio element.
</audio>
```

<video>: Embeds video content.

```
<video width="320" height="240" controls>
  <source src="video.mp4" type="video/mp4">
  Your browser does not support the video element.
</video>
```

5. Forms and Input Types

<form>: Defines an HTML form for user input.

```
<form action="/submit" method="post">
  <label for="name">Name:</label>
```

```
 <input type="text" id="name" name="name">
 <input type="submit" value="Submit">
</form>
```

\<input>: Defines an input control.

```
<input type="email" name="email" placeholder="Enter your email">
```

\<button>: Defines a clickable button.

```
<button type="button">Click Me</button>
```

6. Semantic HTML5 Tags

\<header>: Represents introductory content or navigational links.

```
<header>
 <h1>Site Header</h1>
</header>
```

\<footer>: Represents footer content.

```
<footer>
 <p>&copy; 2024 My Website</p>
</footer>
```

<article>: Represents independent content.

```
<article>
 <h2>Article Title</h2>
 <p>Article content goes here.</p>
</article>
```

<section>: Represents a thematic grouping of content.

```
<section>
 <h2>Section Title</h2>
 <p>Section content.</p>
</section>
```

<nav>: Defines navigation links.

```
<nav>
```

```
  <ul>
    <li><a href="#home">Home</a></li>
    <li><a href="#about">About</a></li>
  </ul>
</nav>
```

Frequently Used Snippets

Responsive Meta Tag

To ensure your website is mobile-friendly, include this meta tag in the **<head>** section:

```
<meta name="viewport" content="width=device-width, initial-scale=1.0">
```

HTML5 Boilerplate

A basic HTML5 template to start your projects:

```
<!DOCTYPE html>
<html lang="en">
<head>
  <meta charset="UTF-8">
  <meta name="viewport" content="width=device-width, initial-scale=1.0">
```

```html
<title>Document Title</title>
<link rel="stylesheet" href="styles.css">
</head>
<body>
<header>
  <h1>Welcome to My Website</h1>
</header>
<main>
  <!-- Main content goes here -->
</main>
<footer>
  <p>&copy; 2024 My Website</p>
</footer>
</body>
</html>
```

Form Validation with Required Fields

Basic form validation to ensure required fields are filled:

```html
<form action="/submit" method="post">
  <label for="name">Name:</label>
  <input type="text" id="name" name="name" required>
  <label for="email">Email:</label>
  <input type="email" id="email" name="email" required>
  <input type="submit" value="Submit">
</form>
```

Adding Placeholder Text

Use placeholder attributes to provide hints within form fields:

```html
<input type="text" id="username" name="username" placeholder="Enter your username">
```

Embedding a Google Map

Embed a Google Map using an iframe:

```html
<iframe
  width="600"
  height="450"
  style="border:0;"
  loading="lazy"
  allowfullscreen
```

```
src="https://www.google.com/maps/embed/v1/place?q=place_id:ChIJN1t_tDeuEmsRUsoyG
83frY4&key=YOUR_API_KEY">
</iframe>
```

Common Tags and Attributes: Includes essential HTML5 elements such as document structure tags, text formatting, links, lists, images, media, and forms.

Frequently Used Snippets: Provides practical examples for common use cases like responsive design, form validation, placeholder text, and embedding external content.

This cheat sheet serves as a quick reference for HTML5 developers, offering a concise overview of key tags, attributes, and code snippets to facilitate efficient and effective web development.

Glossary

A glossary is an essential resource for understanding the terminology used in HTML5 and web development. This section provides definitions for key terms and concepts, helping you grasp the foundational elements and practices in HTML5.

Key Terms and Definitions

HTML (Hypertext Markup Language)

Definition: HTML is the standard markup language used to create and design web pages. It structures content on the web using various tags and attributes.

Example: **<p>This is a paragraph.</p>** – This HTML code defines a paragraph of text on a web page.

HTML5

Definition: HTML5 is the latest version of HTML, introduced to enhance web capabilities with new elements, attributes, and APIs for richer web applications and multimedia.

Example: The `<video>` tag in HTML5 allows embedding video content directly into a web page.

Doctype Declaration

Definition: The `<!DOCTYPE html>` declaration specifies the HTML version and helps browsers render the page correctly. For HTML5, it ensures the document is interpreted as HTML5.

Example: `<!DOCTYPE html>` – Declares the document to be HTML5.

Tags

Definition: Tags are the basic building blocks of HTML used to define and structure content. Tags are enclosed in angle brackets and usually come in pairs (opening and closing).

Example: **<h1>Header</h1>** – The **<h1>** tag defines a top-level heading.

Attributes

Definition: Attributes provide additional information about HTML elements. They are specified in the opening tag and usually come in name-value pairs.

Example: **<a href="https://example.com">Link</a>** – The **href** attribute specifies the URL of the link.

Semantic HTML

Definition: Semantic HTML uses tags that convey the meaning of the content they enclose, improving accessibility and search engine optimization.

Example: `<article>` – Represents a self-contained piece of content that could be distributed independently.

Canvas API

Definition: The Canvas API allows drawing graphics and animations directly in a web page using JavaScript. It provides a way to create complex visual content programmatically.

Example: **<canvas id="myCanvas" width="500" height="500"></canvas>** – Defines an area on the page where graphics can be drawn.

SVG (Scalable Vector Graphics)

Definition: SVG is an XML-based format for creating vector graphics that can be scaled to any size without losing quality. It is used for drawing shapes, paths, and text.

Example: **<svg width="100" height="100"><circle cx="50" cy="50" r="40" stroke="black" stroke-width="3" fill="red" /></svg>** – Creates a red circle inside an SVG container.

Geolocation API

Definition: The Geolocation API allows web applications to access the geographical location of a user's device, such as latitude and longitude.

Example: **navigator.geolocation.getCurrentPosition(successCallback, errorCallback);** – Retrieves the current position of the user.

Web Storage

Definition: Web Storage provides mechanisms for storing data on the client side. It includes Local Storage and Session Storage for managing data persistently and temporarily.

Example: **localStorage.setItem('key', 'value');** – Stores a value in Local Storage.

Responsive Design

Definition: Responsive design ensures that web pages look and function well on various devices and screen sizes by using fluid grids, flexible images, and media queries.

Example: **@media (max-width: 600px) { /* CSS rules for small screens */ }** – Applies styles for devices with a screen width of 600 pixels or less.

ARIA (Accessible Rich Internet Applications)

Definition: ARIA is a set of attributes that enhances the accessibility of web content by providing additional information to assistive technologies.

Example: **aria-label="Close"** – Provides a label for a close button for screen readers.

SEO (Search Engine Optimization)

Definition: SEO is the practice of optimizing web pages to improve their visibility and ranking in search engine results. It involves using keywords, meta tags, and other techniques.

Example: **<meta name="description" content="A brief description of the page">** – Helps search engines understand the content of the page.

Form Validation

Definition: Form validation ensures that user input meets specific criteria before submitting a form. HTML5 offers built-in validation features like required fields and input types.

Example: **<input type="email" required>** – Ensures the user enters a valid email address.

Media Queries

Definition: Media queries are a CSS technique used to apply styles based on the characteristics of the device or viewport, such as screen width or resolution.

Example: **@media screen and (min-width: 768px) { /* CSS rules for screens wider than 768px */ }** – Applies styles for devices with a minimum width of 768 pixels.

Local Storage

Definition: Local Storage is a Web Storage feature that allows data to be stored persistently in a user's browser. Data remains available even after the browser is closed.

Example: **localStorage.setItem('username', 'JohnDoe');** – Stores a username that persists across browser sessions.

Session Storage

Definition: Session Storage is a Web Storage feature that stores data for the duration of a browser session. Data is cleared when the browser or tab is closed.

Example: `sessionStorage.setItem('sessionData', 'value');` – Stores data that is specific to the current session.

Inline vs. Block Elements

Definition: Inline elements do not break the flow of content and appear on the same line, while block elements start on a new line and take up the full width available.

Example: **<span>** (inline) vs. **<div>** (block) – A **<span>** tag will appear within the flow of surrounding text, while a **<div>** tag will start on a new line and extend across the container.

Meta Tags

Definition: Meta tags provide metadata about an HTML document, such as character encoding, viewport settings, and page descriptions.

Example: **<meta charset="UTF-8">** – Specifies the character encoding for the document.

Viewport

Definition: The viewport is the visible area of a web page on a user's device. The viewport meta tag controls how the page is scaled and displayed on different devices.

Example: **<meta name="viewport" content="width=device-width, initial-scale=1.0">** – Ensures the page scales correctly on various devices.

This glossary provides definitions for key HTML5 and web development terms, helping you understand the foundational concepts and terminology used in HTML5. Each term is accompanied by examples to illustrate its practical application and significance in web development.

HTML5 Made Easy

Unlock the power of modern web development with "HTML5 Made Easy," your ultimate guide to mastering HTML5, the cornerstone of contemporary websites and web applications. Whether you're a novice looking to build your first web page or an experienced developer seeking to update your skills, this book provides a clear, comprehensive, and practical approach to HTML5.

What You'll Learn:

- Foundations of HTML5: Understand the evolution, specifications, and features that make HTML5 a game-changer in web development.

- Setting Up Your Environment: Get hands-on guidance on installing text editors and setting up a local server for efficient development.

- Document Structure and Formatting: Master the structure of an HTML5 document, including the crucial Doctype declaration and semantic elements.

- Interactive Elements: Dive into creating links, lists, images, and media to make your web pages engaging and dynamic.

- Advanced Form Handling: Explore the new input types, form validation, and attributes that HTML5 offers for creating robust forms.

- Graphics and Animations: Unleash your creativity with the Canvas API and Scalable Vector Graphics (SVG) for stunning visuals.

- APIs and Storage: Implement powerful features like the Geolocation API and Web Storage to enhance user experiences.

- Styling and Scripting: Integrate CSS3 and JavaScript to style and script your HTML5 documents for rich, interactive web applications.

- Best Practices and SEO: Adopt best practices for writing clean, maintainable code and optimizing your pages for search engines.

- Performance Optimization: Learn techniques to ensure your web applications run smoothly and efficiently.

- Real-World Projects and Case Studies: Apply your knowledge with practical projects, including building a responsive website and exploring HTML5 game development.

- Future Trends: Stay ahead with insights into the future of HTML5 and its evolving landscape.

Why Choose This Book?

- Comprehensive Coverage: From basic concepts to advanced features, this book covers everything you need to know about HTML5.

- Hands-On Approach: Practical examples and projects ensure you can apply what you learn immediately.

- Expert Insights: Benefit from the author's extensive experience and clear, engaging writing style.

"HTML5 Made Easy" is more than just a tutorial; it's a complete resource that will empower you to create modern, responsive, and dynamic web applications with confidence. Begin your journey into the exciting world of HTML5 today!

Grab your copy now and start building the future of the web with HTML5!